Unexploded Ordnance Cleanup Costs

Implications of Alternative Protocols

T0159309

Jacqueline MacDonald, Carmen Mendez

RAND
CORPORATION

This research in the public interest was supported by RAND, using discretionary funds made possible by the generosity of RAND's donors, the fees earned on client-funded research, and independent research and development (IR&D) funds provided by the Department of Defense.

Library of Congress Cataloging-in-Publication Data

MacDonald, Jacqueline.
    Unexploded ordnance cleanup costs : implications of alternative protocols /
Jacqueline MacDonald, Carmen Mendez.
        p. cm.
    "MG-244."
    Includes bibliographical references.
    ISBN 0-8330-3774-9 (pbk.)
    1. Explosive ordnance disposal—United States—Costs. 2. Unexploded
ordnance—Environmental aspects—United States. I. Mendez, Carmen, 1977–
II. Title.

    UF860.M33 2005
    355.4—dc22
                                                            2005006110

The RAND Corporation is a nonprofit research organization providing objective analysis and effective solutions that address the challenges facing the public and private sectors around the world. RAND's publications do not necessarily reflect the opinions of its research clients and sponsors.

RAND˚ is a registered trademark.

Published 2005 by the RAND Corporation
1776 Main Street, P.O. Box 2138, Santa Monica, CA 90407-2138
1200 South Hayes Street, Arlington, VA 22202-5050
201 North Craig Street, Suite 202, Pittsburgh, PA 15213-1516
RAND URL: http://www.rand.org/
To order RAND documents or to obtain additional information, contact
Distribution Services: Telephone: (310) 451-7002;
Fax: (310) 451-6915; Email: order@rand.org

Preface

This monograph documents the findings of a study examining cost estimation for unexploded ordnance (UXO) remediation conducted at closed military installations. With continued military downsizing and base closures, cleanup of UXO at former weapons ranges has become one of the most costly environmental problems the military faces. The research discussed in this monograph examines the difficulties of accurately estimating cleanup costs and the major effects that different cleanup requirements and methods can have on cost. The report assesses previous estimates of UXO cleanup costs and evaluates the strengths and limitations of the military's preferred cost-estimation tool, the Remedial Action Cost Engineering Requirements (RACER) software package. Then, using a modified method for implementing RACER, the monograph shows how costs change depending on which cleanup protocol is followed. The results show that the choice of cleanup protocol has major cost implications.

This monograph should be of interest to Department of Defense officials, Environmental Protection Agency representatives, state regulators, local land use agencies, and citizen groups with concerns about the UXO cleanup process. It also should be of interest to analysts using RACER or attempting cost estimation by other methods. It is part of RAND's program of work on the cleanup and reuse of public land at closed, transferred, and transferring military installations that contain UXO.

This monograph results from the RAND Corporation's continuing program of self-initiated research. Support for such research is provided, in part, by donors and by the independent research and development provisions of RAND's contracts for the operation of its U.S. Department of Defense federally funded research and development centers. The research that led to this monograph was managed by RAND Arroyo Center's Military Logistics Program. RAND Arroyo Center, part of the RAND Corporation, is a federally funded research and development center sponsored by the United States Army.

For more information on RAND Arroyo Center, contact the Director of Operations (telephone 310-393-0411, extension 6419; FAX 310-451-6952; email Marcy_Agmon@rand.org), or visit Arroyo's web site at http://www.rand.org/ard/.

Contents

Figures

Tables

Summary

Military downsizing has resulted in the closure of numerous military bases that once hosted military training and weapons testing activities. Ultimate plans call for many of these former range areas to be transferred or sold to civilians—either to other government agencies or to private landowners. The presence of unexploded ordnance (UXO)—bombs, grenades, rockets, and other munitions that have been primed and launched but failed to detonate—has interfered with efforts to transfer and sell this land because of the potential hazards it poses to civilians. All types of ordnance have a failure rate, ranging from a few percent to 30 percent. As a result, unexploded munitions that could still detonate at some future time are inevitably present on any land where the military has trained with or tested weapons.

The research presented in this monograph explores issues related to the cost of cleaning up UXO.[1] The analysis illustrates that the costs to search for and excavate UXO can vary by orders of magnitude depending upon the process used and the clearance requirements. Since final agreements on these processes and requirements have not been reached at many UXO sites, the estimates of total cleanup costs remain speculative.

---

[1] Throughout this monograph, we use the terms "UXO cleanup," "UXO clearance," "UXO remediation," and "UXO response" interchangeably. In each case, we mean the set of steps taken to reduce the UXO hazard. We realize that at many sites, even after extensive efforts are made to search for and excavate UXO, complete cleanup may not be achieved, and some UXO may remain.

Previous Estimates of UXO Cleanup Costs

In response to requests from Congress, the Department of Defense (DoD) has generated several estimates of the costs it expects to incur in cleaning up UXO at closed or closing domestic military installations in the coming years. These estimates have produced varying results. Some have predicted that costs will total $8 billion, while others project costs of up to $140 billion. The discrepancies in the estimates are due to a lack of complete data on the locations and characteristics of UXO sites, a lack of standard cost-estimation procedures, and a lack of agreement on what cleanup processes will ultimately be required.

DoD is compiling a comprehensive inventory of UXO sites that will contain information necessary for cost estimation. It has also been working on standardizing the cost-estimation process for planning purposes. But even with complete data and a reliable, standard cost-estimation tool, forecasting the total costs may not be possible without further information about what UXO cleanup protocol is satisfactory to protect the public health for different land uses. Without knowing what steps will be taken during UXO cleanup, and the extent of the search for UXO that will be required, it is impossible to forecast costs accurately.

Controversy over UXO Remediation Standards

Currently, there are no enforceable standards for UXO cleanup. Although the DoD Explosives Safety Board (DDESB) released guidelines tying future land use to recommended clearance depth (see Table S.1), these guidelines are not binding. Rather, DoD's directive for UXO clearance, entitled "DoD Ammunition and Explosives Safety Standards," states that the "preferred method to determine remediation depths is to use site-specific information." Thus at each new site, DoD must negotiate a clearance depth with the environmental regulators, state and local officials, and involved citizens. In the absence of

Table S.1
DoD Explosives Safety Board Guidelines for Clearing UXO Sites

Planned End Use	Default Removal Depth
Unrestricted (commercial, residential, construction, subsurface recreational, utility)	10 feet
Public access (farming, agriculture, surface recreational, vehicle parking, surface supply storage)	4 feet
Limited public access (livestock grazing, wildlife preserve)	1 foot
Not yet determined	Surface
Like use	Not applicable

SOURCE: DoD Explosives Safety Board (1999).

enforceable standards, reaching agreement on clearance requirements at each individual site is a time-consuming process.

In addition to disagreeing on clearance depth requirements, DoD, the Environmental Protection Agency (EPA), and state environmental regulatory agencies have been unable to reach consensus on how the search should be conducted. The only available tools for finding UXO are metal detectors, which signal the location of all buried metal, not just UXO but also harmless shrapnel, rocks containing natural iron, coins, cans, and other metallic items. Usually, contractors conduct an initial survey to map the locations of buried metal on a computer database. They then analyze the data to determine which items are most likely to be UXO and return to the site to resurvey with metal detectors and dig up suspicious items. Once this process is completed, there is still some risk that UXO not found by the metal detectors or not flagged for excavation will remain buried.

As a result of the risk of some UXO remaining, the involved parties cannot agree on what set of steps should be taken to ensure that the land is safe for reuse. Suggested protocols range from clearing only the UXO on the ground surface, to surveying the affected area once using the scan-map-scan-dig approach described above, to conducting multiple surveys over the same area or portions of it, to digging up and sifting all the soil. DoD has contended that the latter approach is too costly, while at some installations environmental regulators have contended that the other approaches may not provide an adequate guarantee of public safety (see Chapter Three). For example, at one installation the lead state environmental regulator told us that the state would like DoD to guarantee that the top several feet of soil in areas slated for residential development are 100 percent free of UXO. To provide this guarantee, the state would like DoD to excavate the entire area one foot at a time, with metal detector searches conducted prior to each new one-foot excavation. DoD has rejected this proposal as too costly.

The RACER Cost-Estimation Tool

For this study, we wanted to explore how changes in UXO cleanup protocols (clearance depth, number of surveys with a metal detector, and amount of excavation) could affect costs. To do so, we needed a cost-estimation tool. We chose the software package "Remedial Action Cost Engineering Requirements" (RACER). This software is widely used by DoD to estimate the costs of a range of environmental remediation activities. It includes a module, developed in conjunction with the U.S. Army Corps of Engineers, for estimating UXO cleanup costs.

To better understand the strengths and limitations of RACER and how it might bias the outcomes of our cost computations, we conducted a sensitivity analysis. Its purpose was to identify which input variables have the greatest impact on UXO cleanup cost, according to RACER. As well, we wanted to assess whether RACER included all the potential cost factors we thought were important.

The sensitivity analysis revealed that the input variables that have the most significant influence on cost are total acreage, number of UXO and other metal items per acre, and amount of vegetation that must be cleared before UXO surveys can begin. This was as we expected. However, we also identified some limitations:

- **The extra costs of increasing clearance depth are not well represented.** Most important, RACER does not fully account for the increased costs that may be incurred when greater clearance depths are required. RACER's cost estimates are nearly constant with changes in depth. We were able to devise a RACER implementation strategy (described below) that could partly overcome this deficiency.

- **Soil effects are not considered.** RACER does not account for the effects of soil type on costs. The effort involved in searching for and excavating UXO may vary depending on whether the soil is loose sand or hard-packed clay, and on whether or not it contains a high level of natural iron (which can interfere with the performance of the detection equipment). RACER does not provide a means for estimating the effects of soil type on cost.

- **No option is provided to modify the vegetation removal process.** RACER assumes that the effort required for vegetation removal is the same regardless of the terrain. It offers no capability to specify if the vegetation will be removed by controlled burning, with machinery, or manually.

- **Performance rates are not adjusted to reflect changes in excavation equipment.** RACER assumes that backhoes will be used for all excavation. But personnel at installations with UXO told us that much excavation is done manually, with shovels. RACER allows users to remove the cost of renting backhoes, but it does not accordingly adjust the time or number of personnel required for excavation.

- **Default density values are questionable.** RACER uses default values to estimate UXO density (number of UXOs per unit of land area) based on range type. When site-specific data are available, the user can override the default density values. In the absence of site-specific data, however, RACER's default density estimates are unlikely to be accurate because they do not account for the length of time the range was in use, the amount of ordnance fired, or whether there were changes in the range's use over time.

Despite these limitations, we were able to adapt RACER for our cost analysis, as described below.

Case Study: How UXO Clearance Requirements Affect Costs

Our primary purpose in conducting this study was to consider how changing the processes required for UXO cleanup might affect costs. To explore this question, we analyzed the costs of three different potential UXO cleanup strategies using data from an actual military installation. The installation asked that we keep the name of the site confidential, so we refer to it as Site A. Site A is a former multipurpose military training range that contains about 7,000 acres of rolling, wooded terrain. We chose Site A because a large amount of data on UXO density, topographic characteristics, and vegetation density is available for it.

At Site A, as at many UXO sites, the military and the state cannot agree on what UXO cleanup processes should be used. We analyzed the costs of two of the proposals put forward—one by the military and one by the state—and of a third alternative that represents a compromise.

- Protocol 1, preferred by the military, involves surveying the entire area with metal detectors and then digging up every metal anomaly to a depth of one, two, or four feet. The state objects to this protocol, contending that metal detectors might miss some UXO.

- Protocol 2, suggested by the state for areas that will be developed for residential uses, would involve excavating all the soil in affected areas and sifting it to remove any UXO. Under this proposal, the excavation would proceed in one-foot depth increments, and the ground would be surveyed with a metal detector before each excavation to reduce risks to workers. The military has contended that this approach would be too costly.

- Protocol 3, the possible compromise, would involve carrying out protocol 1 and then surveying the entire area again with a metal detector to locate UXO missed on the first search. More than two surveys might be needed to ensure that as much UXO as possible is located. This protocol would not guarantee that all

UXO has been found, because some items might not be detected at all due to their size, depth, and orientation, but it still could increase the probability of detection.

Our cost analysis probed the financial implications of choosing one or the other of these strategies. Table S.2 summarizes the results for the first two protocols. Table S.3 shows the results for the third protocol. For the third protocol, we assumed a four-foot clearance depth, meaning that search crews would dig up to four feet deep wherever their equipment indicated that UXO might be present. For the others, we calculated costs for four different clearance depths. Figure S.1 summarizes the costs for all the protocols and all the variations within each protocol.

Table S.2
Summary of Costs of Protocols 1 and 2

Depth	Protocol 1 Total Cost ($ Millions)	Protocol 2 Total Cost ($ Millions)
Surface	35	35
1 foot	63	320
2 feet	64	590
4 feet	67	1,100

Table S.3
Summary of Costs of Protocol 3

Number of Full-Site Surveys with Metal Detector (Four-Foot Search Depth)	Total Cost ($ Millions)
1	67
2	84
3	98
4	110
5	120

Figure S.1
Cost Differences Among Alternative UXO Cleanup Protocols at Case Study Site

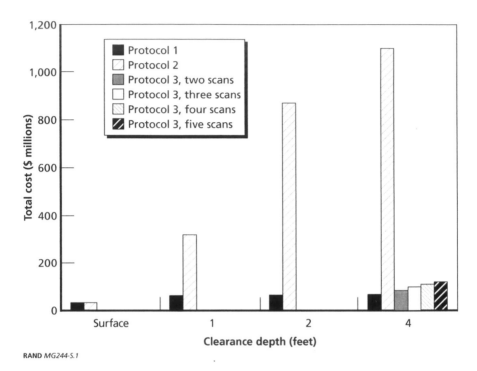

RAND *MG244-S.1*

As Figure S.1 illustrates, the cost differences among the alternatives are very large. The most expensive alternative (protocol 2, with excavation to four feet) would cost DoD $1.1 billion if implemented across all of Site A. This option is more than 30 times as expensive as the least costly alternative (protocol 1 with surface clearance only), which would cost $35 million. The compromise approach of conducting multiple searches with metal detectors without completely excavating the soil would cost $84 million if the entire site were scanned twice and $120 million if it were scanned five times. The total cost of surveying the entire site five times is about one-tenth that required for the excavation and sifting approach.

The budgetary implications of these findings are significant. For example, the entire budget available in fiscal year 2004 for cleaning up all types of environmental contamination at all Army installations closed since the end of the Cold War was $57 million. The cost of cleaning up Site A to any depth below the surface—even using the least costly protocol—exceeds this entire annual budget, which is intended to cover many other installations and kinds of environmental contaminants.

Recommendations for Improving Cost Estimation

Changes in cost estimation and budgeting are needed to allow DoD to effectively plan how it will resolve the UXO problem. In particular, we recommend the following steps.

1. DoD should continue its efforts to develop a uniform strategy for UXO cleanup cost estimation. A feasible way to reach this goal is to modify RACER's OE [ordnance and explosives] Removal Action Module and to establish a standardized RACER implementation method.

2. DoD should work with its contractors to improve RACER's ability to estimate UXO cleanup costs. In particular, RACER needs the following additional capabilities:

   • accurate calculation of cost estimates for different search depth requirements, considering the vertical distribution of UXO;

   • consideration of how soil type affects costs;

   • inclusion of the length of time a range was used for different weapons activities in the calculation of default values for anomaly density;

   • an option to select the method for vegetation clearance (manual, mechanical, or controlled burn) and to choose the method for ordnance excavation (backhoes or shovels); and

   • an option to disable the automatic return to default settings when changes are made to the "Removal Area" tab.

3. DoD and its contractors should conduct an exercise to calibrate and validate the modified RACER OE Removal Module. Once initial modifications are completed, the OE Removal Module should be validated by checking it against actual cost data for a variety of different types of UXO sites. Then it should be modified again as necessary to correct additional limitations identified in the validation process.

Recommendations for Improving Government Management of UXO Sites

Due to the multiple limitations and challenges associated with UXO remediation efforts, solving the UXO problem involves more than a simple decision to clean up the land. No existing technology can guarantee that all UXO has been located, and as a result, regulators and the military have had difficulty agreeing on what UXO clearance process is sufficient to protect the public. The federal government should prepare a plan for developing baseline UXO clearance standards to end the stalemates that have arisen at many installations among regulators, community members, and the military. In particular, we recommend the following actions.

1. The federal government should designate an executive agency (the Army Corps of Engineers, EPA, or both) to develop baseline standards for UXO clearance. The standards should be tied to future land use and should be flexible enough to account for unique situations but broad enough to recognize the many similarities across sites. A risk assessment algorithm that considers site characteristics (UXO density, depth, and others) and future land uses could be created to guide the decisionmaking process. Sites that deviate significantly from any such classification of site characteristics could be addressed on a case-by-case basis. At a minimum, the standards should specify the search depth required for different land uses. The standards should also

include provisions for periodic reinspection of any sites where some UXO items may have been left behind.

2. The federal government should establish a publicly accessible database of UXO accidents in the United States. As the database matures, the information it contains could be used to update UXO clearance standards. The database should include all domestic UXO incidents, both those that involve explosive ordnance disposal contractors and military personnel and those that involve civilians. It should also include incidents that occur off of military property, such as when UXO is transported from a military installation and causes harm elsewhere. Such a database would provide valuable new information to support estimates of the costs and risks of domestic UXO. The Army Corps of Engineers recently compiled data on UXO incidents involving civilians. However, the data are incomplete because only about half of the known UXO sites were included, and incidents involving military personnel were excluded.

3. The federal government should consider the funding implications of different choices about "how clean is clean enough" for UXO remediation. As shown in this document, UXO clearance can be very costly, and variations in the cleanup protocol can significantly affect the expense of the operation. Given the many uncertainties in calculating UXO cleanup costs, as described in this monograph, new studies would be required to assess how different UXO clearance standards affect costs.

Acknowledgments

We are greatly indebted to the DoD officials at "Site A" for their generosity in providing us with the information necessary to complete this study. Also, we thank those at the RACER helpline for their numerous responses to our queries. We thank the RAND Summer Associate Program for helping to support research on this project during the summer of 2002. We are grateful to Megan Abbott, RAND research communicator, for her assistance in preparing the initial draft of this manuscript and for her helpful editorial suggestions. Thanks also to Adrienn Lanczos for preparing the final manuscript. Most importantly, we thank John Dumond, past director of RAND Arroyo Center's Military Logistics Program, for his continuing encouragement to conduct this and other research related to UXO.

Abbreviations

BRAC	Base Realignment and Closure
CERCLA	Comprehensive Environmental Response, Compensation, and Liability Act
CTT	Closed, transferred, and transferring
DDESB	Department of Defense Explosives Safety Board
DoD	Department of Defense
DSB	Defense Science Board
EPA	Environmental Protection Agency
FUDS	Formerly used defense site
GAO	General Accounting Office
NDAI	No DoD action indicated
OE	Ordnance and explosives
OSHA	Occupational Safety and Health Administration
OSWER	Office of Solid Waste and Emergency Response (Environmental Protection Agency)
RACER	Remedial Action Cost Engineering Requirements
USACE	U.S. Army Corps of Engineers
UXO	Unexploded ordnance

CHAPTER ONE

Introduction: UXO Problem on American Soil

At the end of the Cold War, the U.S. military began a drawdown that resulted in several cycles of military base closures throughout the country. Since 1988, the Department of Defense (DoD) has closed nearly 100 major military installations and many smaller ones (GAO, 2002a). These closures were carried out under the Base Realignment and Closure (BRAC) program, a congressionally mandated initiative aimed at reducing the military's domestic infrastructure and freeing up funds for military modernization (GAO, 2002a).

Under BRAC, land that was once host to training ranges for such activities as firing practice and weapons testing is prepared for transfer to civilian ownership.[1] As DoD relinquishes them, other federal agencies are given first choice of these properties. Any remaining land then becomes available to state and local governments for conversion to schools, parks, commercial or industrial districts, airports, or other uses. Land unclaimed by state and local governments is offered for public sale (GAO, 2002a).

While the BRAC base closures were unprecedented in scale, the military had previous experience in closing small installations. Some 9,000 smaller properties once used by the military are now owned by civilians (U.S. Army Corps of Engineers, 2003b). Properties that DoD relinquished before the BRAC program began are known as "formerly used defense sites" (FUDS).

---

[1] DoD defines a training range as any land mass or water body that is used or was used for conducting training, research, development, testing, or evaluation of military munitions or explosives (GAO, 2001).

Transfers of BRAC and FUDS properties outside the military have not been without complications. Due to their prior use as training ranges, many of these former bases occupy land that, unless it is cleaned up, is unsafe for civilian use. While weapon development and training are necessary military activities, the land on which they are conducted can contain the threat of old but intact munitions, or unexploded ordnance (UXO). Unfortunately, the cleanup of UXO in preparation for the transfer of former military land to civilians has proved technically challenging and extraordinarily expensive. Even defining the extent of the area containing UXO has proved difficult, and the total number of acres affected by UXO remains highly uncertain. These challenges make reliable estimates of cleanup costs crucial to the decisionmaking process, from the prioritization of sites targeted for remediation to the choice of cleanup procedures. This monograph thus focuses on methods for estimating UXO cleanup costs and the effects that various cleanup approaches can have on these costs.

UXO Is Inevitable in Weapons Testing and Training

The term "UXO" refers to any kind of munition that was fired but failed to explode upon impact; it can also refer to buried but long-forgotten weapons caches or disposal sites. Types of UXO found on domestic ranges span the full array of ammunition employed on the battlefield, including tank shells, artillery rounds, bombs, rockets, missiles, mortars, hand grenades, rifle grenades, bulk explosives, detonators, aircraft cannon, torpedoes, mines, pyrotechnics, chemical munitions, submunitions, and small-arms ammunition. Figure 1.1 shows an example of an unexploded mortar found at Fort McClellan during cleanup in preparation for closure, long after the weapon was launched.

Much if not most UXO results from the failure of weapons fired during testing or training to detonate, due either to a malfunction in the arming process or to operator error (Army Environmental Center

Figure 1.1
Fuzed Stokes Mortar Found at Fort McClellan

RAND *MG244-1.1*
SOURCE: UXOInfo.com, Ordnance/UXO photo gallery.

and Army Technical Center for Explosives Safety, 2000). On average, the failure rate in the field is about 10 percent (Defense Science Board, 1998). However, these rates vary with the type of ordnance and even with the particular batch of ordnance. Table 1.1 shows the variation in dud rates during quality control tests conducted by the Army's Ammunition Stockpile Reliability Program (Army Environmental Center and Army Technical Center for Explosives Safety, 2000). Actual dud rates in the field are significantly higher than those shown in Table 1.1, given the possibility of human errors, such as failure to remove the safety pin or to aim the weapon properly. For example, studies in Laos and Cambodia after the Vietnam War indicated that 10 to 30 percent of bombs that the United States dropped on these countries failed to detonate (Lauritzen, 2001). Nonetheless, Table 1.1 illustrates that even under ideal, carefully controlled test

Table 1.1
Average Dud Rates During Quality Control Testing

Munitions Family	Average Dud Rate (%)
Grenade	1.78
Gun	4.68
Howitzer	3.75
Mortar	2.91
Recoilless rifle	3.40
Rocket	3.84
Submunitions	8.23

SOURCE: Army Environmental Center and Army
Technical Center for Explosives Safety (2000).
NOTE: These rates represent carefully controlled test
conditions. During actual field use, dud rates are
much higher due to factors such as failure to aim
properly or to remove the safety pin.

conditions, dud rates are significant and are variable across ordnance types.

The UXO danger stems not only from these detonation failures but also from a lack of record-keeping. According to the Army Technical Center for Explosives Safety, "for troop practice firings at training sites, there is normally no record of number of rounds fired vs. number of duds" (Army Environmental Center and Army Technical Center for Explosives Safety, 2000).

UXO Presents Explosion and Contamination Risks

As long as UXO is in the ground, the risk of someone disturbing the munition and causing an unexpected explosion remains. An Environmental Protection Agency (EPA) survey of records from 203 inactive, closed, transferred, and transferring ranges documented UXO incidents at 24 different facilities. Two incidents led to injuries, and three resulted in fatalities (DoD/EPA, 2000). An EPA review of accident reports in the DoD Explosives Safety Board database and news accounts found reports of 65 UXO-related civilian deaths and 131 dismemberments since World War II.[2] The Army Corps of Engineers in 2003 compiled a list of reported UXO incidents involving civilians at about half of the known UXO sites (U.S. Army Corps of Engineers, 2003a). The contractor found documentation of 102 civilian victims (38 deaths and 64 injuries) between 1913 and 2002. Such reports, however, are only anecdotal. The total number of injuries caused by UXO on U.S. soil is unknown, because there is no comprehensive database of domestic UXO incidents.

UXO poses especially great risks to children, who are unaware of the danger and may mistake the item for a toy. In 1983, for instance, two young boys were killed when they found and began playing with an unexploded 37-millimeter high explosives shell they found in an open space at the end of a cul de sac in their neighborhood. The ordnance had been fired forty years before by a Navy crew training in the Camp Elliott firing range ("Old Firing Range Swept for Shells After Two Die," *New York Times*, January 20, 1984, p. A13). Although such occurrences are uncommon, DoD's Defense Science Board Task Force on UXO predicts that casualties will increase as civilians gain access to closed bases (Defense Science Board, 1998).

Explosion may be the most apparent danger from UXO, but there is a more covert threat from munitions constituents leaking into the ground. Primarily derived from explosives (although lead may also be a hazard at small-arms ranges), munitions constituents include residue resulting from a munition that has partially detonated, the open burning of excess explosives, the corrosion of UXO items, and the breakage of munitions without detonation (Jenkins et al., 2002). Common explosives that may remain in soil at former military training sites include trinitrotoluene (TNT), royal demolition explosive (RDX), high-melting explosive (HMX), and various isomers of dinitrotoluene (DNT). For example, researchers recently sampled soil from six military installations, identifying various combinations of explosives on portions of the ranges. The concentrations of explosives

---

[2] This information is from unpublished data provided by Ken Shuster, Environmental Protection Agency, on August 28, 2000.

varied with the types of ordnance fired (e.g., artillery, grenade, anti-tank), the environmental conditions, and the density of ordnance items. While the concentrations found in the study were generally low and decreased even more with greater distance from the target areas, most ranges did have localized sources with high concentrations (Jenkins et al., 2002).

This Research Focuses on UXO Remediation Costs

This monograph examines the difficulties of estimating UXO cleanup costs and the major effects that different cleanup requirements can have on cost. Chapter Two reviews previous cost estimates and explains why they have been controversial. Chapter Three discusses the lack of adequate technologies for locating buried UXO and how this has fueled a controversy over what cleanup standards should apply, in turn increasing the difficulty of cost estimation. Chapter Four analyzes a software package known as the Remedial Action Cost Engineering Requirements (RACER), which DoD often uses for cleanup cost estimates. The chapter evaluates RACER's sensitivity to variations in input data in order to determine its strengths and limitations for UXO cost estimation. Chapter Five presents a case study analyzing the difference in cost between a UXO cleanup approach proposed by a state regulatory agency and an approach preferred by DoD. Finally, Chapter Six presents our recommendations about steps that need to be taken to improve the accuracy of future UXO cost forecasts.

CHAPTER TWO

Previous Estimates of UXO Cleanup Costs

The costs of UXO cleanup at the nation's closed military installations threaten to overwhelm the DoD environmental budget—and indeed the costs of many other environmental restoration activities across the nation. Previous cost estimates have ranged from approximately $8 billion to $140 billion (see Table 2.1). These amounts are approximately two to thirty times as high as the $4.2 billion 2003 budget allocated to cover all of DoD's environmental programs, from compliance with environmental laws at active bases, to research on pollution prevention, to cleanup of hazardous wastes and UXO at closed bases. So even if all other DoD environmental programs were put on hold and all funding were devoted exclusively to UXO, from two to thirty years would be required to clean up all the UXO sites, according to previous estimates.

In the face of overwhelming remediation costs and budgets that cannot sustain them, policymakers need to plan and prioritize UXO

Table 2.1
Previous Estimates of UXO Remediation Costs at Closed, Transferred, and Transferring Ranges

Estimate Date	Estimated UXO Remediation Cost	Source of Estimate
March 2001	$11.5–$84.2 billion	DoD (2001a)
March 2001	$14 billion	DoD (2001b)
April 2001	$40–$140 billion	GAO (2001)
April 2003	$8–$35 billion	DoD (2003)

remediation with great care. Reliable cost-estimating tools and accurate cost estimates are crucial for planning. Previous attempts to estimate UXO remediation costs, however, have generated controversy. Insufficient data on the number and acreage of sites, the lack of a standard cost-estimating process, and disagreements about which cleanup requirements ultimately will be enforced have made it difficult to prepare reliable and widely accepted cost estimates. Due to these difficulties, previous cost estimates have varied by an order of magnitude, depending on the assumptions and cost-estimating procedures underlying the analysis. This chapter discusses previous calculations of UXO cleanup costs at closed installations and the major reasons for the uncertainty in the resulting numbers.

Congress Required an Estimate of UXO Costs

In the National Defense Authorization Act of 2000, the U.S. Senate included a provision requiring the Secretary of Defense to submit a report to congressional defense committees with an estimate of the current and projected costs of UXO remediation at closed, transferred, and transferring (CTT) installations as well as active facilities.[1] In response, DoD began an evaluation of the costs associated with the UXO cleanup effort. In March 2001, DoD submitted its results in a report titled *Unexploded Ordnance Response, Technology, and Costs*. In this document, DoD reported a baseline estimate of $14 billion for the cost of UXO remediation at closed, transferred, and transferring ranges. Prior DoD projections, however, had estimated that costs could potentially be much higher. In fact, in a preliminary report to Congress—which was later retracted and replaced by the final report mentioned above—DoD estimated that costs would range from

---

[1] At active ranges, DoD regulations require that the Army periodically clear all UXO found on the surface. This is a minimal cleanup activity compared to the kind needed for transfer of the land to public use. Furthermore, we were told that this regulation is not always obeyed.

$11.5 billion to $84.2 billion for cleaning up all CTT ranges (DoD, 2001a, Section 4-5).

The large disparity between the two estimates resulted from the use of different assumptions and cost computation methods—the consequences of a general lack of standardization of approach. The difficulties encountered in generating these estimates illustrate the considerable obstacles that analysts confront in attempting to generate robust UXO remediation cost estimates.

Initial DoD Estimate Used Centralized Approach

To prepare its initial estimate (the $11.5–$84.2 billion range for all CTT sites that was later withdrawn) DoD attempted to centralize the analytical process by collecting a new set of site-specific data and approaching the cost-estimating process via a specific methodology and basic set of assumptions. First, DoD surveyed the military components (Army, Navy, and Air Force) about the number and acreage of ranges where munitions have been used. Data gathered for this baseline survey included land uses, site characteristics such as topography, and types of ordnance fired at the site. The data collected included 4,033 ranges that *could* contain UXO—all CTT and active installations included.[2] The total land area considered in these estimates was 23,151,653 acres, out of which 5,704,768 acres were CTT sites. The cost estimators assumed that for each range, anywhere from 5 to 75 percent of the total acreage contained UXO. Based on historical information, they assumed a 95 percent probability that the acreage requiring UXO cleanup would be less than 20 percent of the total range acreage.

Once site-specific data were complete, DoD analysts entered the information into RACER to estimate the total national costs of UXO response. Due to all the uncertainties involved in the data and in the cost-estimating process more generally, DoD generated a cost range instead of a point estimate. To develop the range of values, analysts used a statistical procedure known as Monte Carlo sampling. In the

---

[2] The cost estimate for all CTT and active/inactive ranges was $106.9–$391.5 billion.

Monte Carlo process, values for input variables are randomly selected (from a probability distribution representing the range of possible values) and entered into the cost model. This process is repeated multiple times to generate a cost curve. This curve showed a potential cost range of $11.5–$84.2 billion for CTT ranges, with a most likely value of $41.4 billion.

In its conclusions, the preliminary cost report noted that DoD would take steps to improve its future cost estimates. Acknowledging the "uncertainty and complexity of the UXO response process," DoD asserted its commitment to improving the cost-estimating process by obtaining better site-specific data, refining the cost-estimating tool, accounting for new technological improvements, and developing a strong UXO management program.

Initial DoD Estimate Was Withdrawn and Replaced

A few months after its completion, the preliminary report was withdrawn and replaced with a new one. DoD explained that the wrong acreage had been used for the initial cost estimate. The substitute document, featuring the same title and date, reported a new cost estimate of $14 billion for UXO remediation of CTT ranges, as compared with the original $11.5–$84.2 billion estimated cost range and $41.4 billion most likely cost. Table 2.2 compares the two estimates.

While not as detailed as the preliminary version in documenting the assumptions underlying the estimate, the final report explained that the $14 billion estimate was based on the FY 2000 financial statements from the Army, Navy, and Air Force. Each service developed its own cost estimates, using varied methods. The Army used the aforementioned RACER. The Navy and the Air Force used broad assumptions from preliminary regulatory impact analyses, although the report does not identify what these assumptions were or how the Navy and Air Force used them for their estimates. The combination of all three estimates comprises the $14 billion reported cost.

Referring to it as "the best estimate available in FY 2000," the final report acknowledges that the $14 billion figure is neither comprehensive nor based on a standard methodology and that DoD is in

Table 2.2
Preliminary Versus Final DoD Cost Estimates for UXO Remediation at Closed, Transferred, and Transferring Ranges

	Preliminary Estimate	Final Estimate
Acreage	5,704,768 acres	Not specified
Acreage source	DoD baseline survey specific for the estimate	Not specified
Methodology	• Centralized across DoD • Based on site-specific data • Used RACER as cost-estimating tool • Used consistent assumptions for all sites	• Army, Air Force, and Navy generated their own cost estimates independently, with varied methods • Independent cost estimates were combined to obtain DoD total
Cost	$11.5–$84.2 billion	$14 billion

the process of developing a "consistent, standardized, and defensible cost-estimation methodology." Such a process, the report notes, will include an independent validation of the UXO portion of the RACER cost-estimating tool, a comprehensive inventory of all the DoD ranges, estimates of the percentage of ranges likely to be UXO contaminated, consideration of likely cleanup requirements, and development of a better understanding of the effect of chemical constituents on soil and water (DoD, 2001b).

As these reports and their divergent findings demonstrate, many uncertainties underlie the UXO cleanup effort, making accurate cost estimates difficult to achieve. The two primary reasons for the discrepancy between DoD's previous estimates were the lack of (1) site-specific data and (2) a standard cost-estimation method. As noted earlier, the preliminary report intended to centralize the cost-estimation process by collecting a new set of site-specific data and approaching the cost-estimating process via a specific methodology and basic set of assumptions. The inherent limits of the data, however, led to a possible overestimate of the total acreage requiring UXO remediation. Likewise, the final official report is constrained by the fact that it combines the cost estimates developed independently by the

Army, Air Force, and Navy, each of which used a different method. The latter estimate thus suffers from a lack of consistency in the way the data were collected and in the way the estimates were generated. Further, this latter estimate provides only a point value rather than a possible cost range, thus failing to reflect the considerable uncertainty in the estimate.

GAO Review Criticized DoD's Estimate

In April 2001, the U.S. General Accounting Office (GAO) presented a report to the chair of the House Committee on the Budget in which it evaluated the final DoD estimate. The report stated that the $14 billion figure DoD conveyed to Congress was likely understated. The report noted that "other DoD estimates show that its liability for training range cleanup could exceed $100 billion." The report cited interviews in which DoD officials said that previous, in-house cost estimates ranged from $40 billion to $140 billion. The report noted, "Without complete and accurate data, it is impossible to determine whether these amounts represent a reasonable estimate of the long-term budget implications of cleaning up DoD's training ranges" (GAO, 2001, p. 5).

The GAO report stressed the need for an accurate and complete training range inventory and a consistent cost-estimation method, noting that DoD did not issue formal guidance to the Army, Air Force, and Navy for collecting the necessary information. As a result, the services used different methods to estimate the size and condition of their ranges and to estimate their liability costs. For example, the GAO report noted the disjuncture between the Navy and Air Force methods. The Navy estimated its acreage based on limited surveys completed from 1995 to 1997 and applied a cleanup cost of $10,000 per acre; meanwhile, the Air Force estimated its number of closed ranges and applied historical costs from other cleanup efforts. The Army, in turn, used different methods for transferred ranges than for closed ranges (GAO, 2001). This lack of standardization, according to GAO, calls into question the reliability of the estimate and high-lights the need for a consistent method and complete data.

As we were finishing this monograph, the DoD issued a revised cost estimate. The new figures estimated that the costs of UXO remediation at CTT installations would range from $8 billion to $35 billion (DoD, 2003). The GAO had not issued a review of this estimate at the time our work was being completed.

Site Inventory Was Lacking in Previous Estimates

It is not surprising that the DoD had difficulty in generating a cost estimate, because the most basic piece of information required for the computation—an inventory of affected sites—was not available at the time. In 2002, Congress, in part because of the need for improved cost information, mandated that DoD prepare a comprehensive database of all its current and former ranges by May 31, 2003. Preparation of this inventory is under way, but the data are not yet complete. As of the end of 2002, the inventory contained 2,307 sites known or suspected to contain UXO (DoD, 2003). When the inventory is finished, a detailed report will be available for each known CTT installation, describing the installation history, munitions uses and locations over time, and specific data for each area that may contain UXO. These data will include past uses, UXO types, proximity to drinking water sources, depth to groundwater, and UXO density (on a scale of low, medium, or high).

Still, uncertainties will remain even with a centralized inventory of known ranges. There is always the chance that additional ranges will be discovered in the future. Indeed, many old training ranges—known as "formerly used defense sites" (FUDS)—closed prior to the BRAC initiative have been identified by accident. For example, in 1993, a contractor digging a utility trench in the Spring Valley area of Washington, D.C., uncovered a disposal pit containing 141 UXO items. Unbeknownst to the current land owners, the area had been used after World War I for chemical weapons disposal (Jaffe, 2000; Nielson, 2002).

Conclusion: The Lack of a Standard Method and Data Have Confounded Cost Estimation

Previous attempts to develop UXO cleanup cost estimates highlight the difficulty of obtaining accurate numbers. In order to generate a reliable estimate, a standard, validated method for cost estimation is necessary. As will be discussed in detail in Chapter Four, DoD has attempted to do so via the development of the RACER cost-estimating tool, but despite its availability, this tool was not universally employed in developing the past estimates.

Moreover, the lack of available data introduces substantial uncertainty into the cost-estimation process. DoD's in-progress comprehensive database of all UXO sites is intended to address this limitation. If the effort is successful, future cost estimates will be much more reliable, but at present analysts must accommodate for deficits in the available data.

In addition to these impediments, a critical limiting factor is the lack of national (or even state) standards for UXO cleanup, as the next chapter discusses. Major policy questions remain about what amount of searching a site for UXO and digging up suspicious objects is enough to declare a site "clean."

CHAPTER THREE

Discord over UXO Remediation Standards

Even if a complete UXO site inventory and a standard cost-estimation procedure were available, development of accurate cost estimates under current regulatory rules would still be constrained by the absence of standards regarding the end-goal of UXO remediation. That is, how does one know when cleanup is complete? Congress has dictated that former bases must undergo UXO remediation in order to be transferred to civilian use. But while DoD carries the ultimate responsibility for the cleanup effort, and therefore the associated monetary costs, the decision to declare a site environmentally clean lies under joint jurisdiction among the military, the EPA, and state environmental agencies. As might be expected, this arrangement can result in conflicts among regulators and DoD representatives, who may disagree in their expectations about both the cost and the effort involved in the remediation process.

This chapter discusses a primary underlying cause of the disagreements over cleanup standards: the absence of adequate technologies for detecting UXO. Environmental regulators and DoD officials have proposed a number of strategies for overcoming these technological limitations but have been unable to agree on which of them is sufficient to protect the public health.

DDESB Directive Is Misunderstood by Regulators

In 1999, the DoD Explosives Safety Board (DDESB) published a directive with general guidelines for UXO clearance. The directive includes a table of recommended depths to which UXO should be removed for different land uses (see Table 3.1). The recommended depths are intended to serve as the starting point for planning UXO cleanup, but the directive states that "the preferred method to determine remediation depths is to use site-specific information." The directive, however, has not been widely accepted by federal and state environmental regulators and thus has been of limited use. Further, environmental regulators often misinterpret the recommended removal depths shown in Table 3.1 as binding. The EPA has formally complained that the DoD does not adhere to the recommended depths; an April 1999 memo from EPA to DoD stated, "DDESB . . . standards for depth of clearance generally are not being followed" (Fields, 1999). As an example, the EPA memo noted, "at Fort Ritchie a surface clearance is proposed for a residential area."

The hesitancy to accept DoD decisions about UXO cleanup is partly a result of the inability to prove that all UXO to a specified depth has been detected and removed. No available detection technology can guarantee that all UXO has been found and eliminated. As a result, regulators and DoD disagree on how UXO clearance should proceed: what process should be used to search for the UXO,

Table 3.1
DoD Explosives Safety Board Guidelines for Clearing UXO Sites

Planned End Use	Default Removal Depth
Unrestricted (commercial, residential, construction, subsurface recreational, utility)	10 feet
Public access (farming, agriculture, surface recreational, vehicle parking, surface supply storage)	4 feet
Limited public access (livestock grazing, wildlife preserve)	1 foot
Not yet determined	Surface
Like use	Not applicable

SOURCE: DoD Explosives Safety Board (1999).

how many times the site should be searched, how the quality of the search should be verified, how deep the search needs to penetrate, and so on. For example, if a metal detector used to locate UXO misses 20 percent of ordnance items, then how does one define a successful clearance to ten feet, knowing that even if all detected anomalies were excavated to that depth, some may have been overlooked? Further, as will be discussed later in this chapter, the military and EPA have been unable to agree on whether the cleanup process should proceed according to the regulatory guidelines of the Comprehensive Environmental Response, Compensation, and Liability Act (CERCLA), which governs cleanup of other kinds of hazardous waste sites.

Technological Limitations Increase Controversy

If there were a technology that could "see" underground and accurately identify all buried objects, then the controversy over UXO cleanup requirements would be more easily solved. Unfortunately, no such technology exists. Instead, clearance crews must rely on metal detectors to try to locate UXO.

To understand why technological limitations have complicated the establishment of UXO cleanup goals, it is necessary to understand the cleanup process. Initially, a team thins or clears any vegetation in the area using mechanical methods or controlled burning. Next, the crew divides the area into grids and splits the grids into approximately one-meter-wide lanes, which are sometimes marked with ropes. The crew then proceeds to look for buried UXO, scanning the land with a hand-held or cart-mounted metal detector (see Figure 3.1). When the detector signals an anomaly, a crew member places a flag on the area to mark it for later excavation or further investigation (Figure 3.1).

Until recently, metal-containing areas signaled by the detector (anomalies) were marked only with flags, and the flagged areas generally were all excavated to check for UXO. However, under the current state-of-the-art practice, the signals emitted by the detector and the geographic locations of the signals are entered into a computer database. Later, trained technicians analyze the detector responses

Figure 3.1
Searching for UXO with a Hand-Held Metal Detector at Fort McClellan

RAND MG244-3.1
SOURCE: Ron Levy, Fort McClellan.

collected to identify, based on characteristics of the signal data, which locations are most likely to contain UXO, rather than harmless metal objects. A "dig list" of these high-probability anomalies is then developed. The field crew then returns to these specific anomalies, excavates and identifies each item (whether or not it is UXO), and searches again with a metal detector to insure that no items were hidden by the signal of the removed items. If required, additional anomalies are excavated and identified.

If the crew uncovers a UXO item, they detonate it in place if it is safe to do so. If not, they carefully remove it and transport it for controlled detonation elsewhere. Once all the suspect areas have been investigated, with metal objects removed and UXO items destroyed, a quality assurance team resurveys a portion of the site. Typically, they might scan about 10 percent of the land again to assess the degree to which the response team has detected and removed potential UXO items.

Metal detectors have several shortcomings as the primary tool for UXO searches. Factors such as the tuning of the detector, the amount of metal content in and burial depth of the ordnance, the orientation (vertical, horizontal, or angled) of the ordnance, and the area's soil type all affect a detector's performance. In addition, the operator's health (e.g., hearing ability and attention span) influences the probability of finding UXO. Problems in the operator's personal life and drinking behavior also affect the outcome (C.H. Heaton, Weston Solutions, Inc., personal communication, 2003).

Another problem with metal detectors as UXO remediation tools is that they produce a very high number of false alarms. Items such as shrapnel (of which there is a large amount at former firing ranges), metal scrap from targets, hubcaps, cans, belt buckles, wire, and rocks containing iron make up most of the "finds" of UXO clearance crews. The state-of-the-art geophysical mapping and data analysis tools now used to help sort through the metal detector signals have markedly decreased the false alarm rate, but it is still extremely high. According to DoD, as many as 99 percent of the objects excavated are nonhazardous metal items (DoD, 2001b, p. 4). At one installation, crews reported to us that they had unearthed approximately 5.5 million items, of which only 49,000, or less than 1 percent, were UXO.

False alarm rates, given the limits of contemporary detectors, are in part a function of operator skill. Because the metal detector can be tuned to different detection levels, the operator's task is to find a balance between tuning the detector too finely, leading to a large number of false alarms, and not finely enough, leading to a failure to detect buried UXO.

A recent study sought to assess metal detector performance in finding UXO (Parsons Engineering Science, Inc., 2002). Researchers found that in a controlled, laboratory setting, most of the metal detectors tested were able to signal the presence of the majority of the ordnance types planted to depths of two feet or less. Some detectors were also able to locate larger ordnance at greater depths. However, when tests were conducted at the site itself rather than in a controlled environment, the results were quite different. For the field trials, metal detectors were used to search areas contaminated with UXO from actual military training. Then, the soil at the site was excavated and sifted to determine the percentage of UXO items detected. The results were disappointing. Figure 3.2 shows the probability of finding UXO within a 1.6-foot radius of the detector signal as a function of the false alarm rate for the six detectors tested at one sector of this field site. As the figure shows, some detectors performed better than others, but the best-performing detector found only about 65 percent

Figure 3.2
Probability of Finding UXO Within 1.6 Feet of a Signal at a Field Site

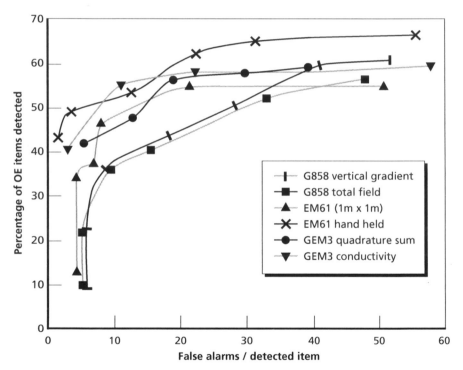

RAND *MG244-3.2*

SOURCE: Parsons Engineering Science, Inc. (2002).

NOTE: The performance of six different detectors (each represented by a different curve) is shown here. For each detector, the detection probability increases as the false alarm rate increases.

of the UXO, even at very high false alarm rates. Results for the other sectors were similar.

The fact that the metal detectors in this study were not very effective in locating UXO buried below two feet is also problematic. As shown in Table 3.2, some UXO, depending on the type of munition, the soil type, and the amount of vegetation at the site, can penetrate to depths of more than 20 feet.

Research to develop better methods for UXO detection is under way. For example, recent innovations have combined geographic information systems with metal detectors to provide a means for the operator to submit field data to a central database in real time. This capability generates a centralized repository of anomaly location data to be analyzed later, and it may reduce the time invested in digging up anomalies. However, these geophysical techniques still rely on the metal detector technology as the basis for locating UXO. As yet, no innovation has been discovered that can replace or transform these detectors and, in so doing, accurately locate all buried UXO with a reasonable false alarm rate (MacDonald et al., 2003).

Table 3.2
Ordnance Penetration Depths

| Munition Type | Ordnance Item | Penetration Depth (feet) | | | |
		Limestone	Sand	Soil Containing Plants	Clay
Projectile	155mm M107	2.0	14.0	18.4	28.0
Projectile	75mm M48	0.7	4.9	6.5	9.9
Projectile	37mm M63	0.6	3.9	5.2	7.9
Grenade	40mm M822	0.5	3.2	4.2	6.4
Projectile	105mm M1	1.1	7.7	10.1	15.4
Rocket	2.36-in rocket	0.1	0.5	0.4	0.8

SOURCE: EPA (2001), as compiled from Army Corps of Engineers and Navy explosive ordnance disposal data.

Regulators Propose Varying Strategies to Compensate for Technical Limitations

To compensate for the fact that metal detectors cannot find all UXO, regulators and DoD have proposed an array of strategies to limit the search costs and/or increase the probability of detection. Among the UXO cleanup strategies that the DoD and regulators have suggested are:

- clearing only surface ordnance;
- excavating anomalies found by the detector to a specified depth (the aforementioned approach recommended by the DDESB and shown in Table 3.1);
- excavating wherever the detector signals until an anomaly is found (regardless of depth);
- excavating wherever the detector signals until an anomaly is found, then scanning the bottom of the resulting hole and excavating again if the detector signals that another anomaly may be present;
- repeating the scan-and-excavate approach multiple times (i.e., searching the site more than once to find UXO missed during the first survey); and
- excavating the entire site to various depths and sifting the excavated soil through a sieve.

Figure 3.3 illustrates the last, most rigorous option. We call this proposed process the "sifting" method. It proceeds as follows:

- All surface UXO is removed, and the site is scanned with a metal detector for the first time. All detected anomalies are excavated, but only up to the first foot of depth.
- Then, the entire first foot layer of soil is removed and sifted through a sieve to ensure the removal of any UXO that the metal detector did not find.
- The bottom of the excavated area, which is now the new surface level of the site, is scanned with the metal detector, removing all

Figure 3.3
"Sifting" Cleanup Protocol

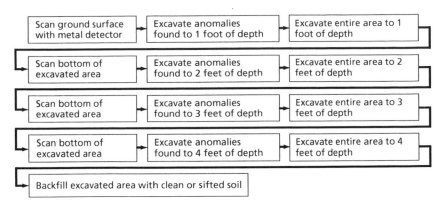

RAND *MG244-3.3*

anomalies up to one additional foot. Then, the second one-foot layer of soil is removed.

- The process is repeated continuously until the specific goal depth for the site is reached, or until no additional items are found.
- Finally, the resulting hole is refilled with the sifted soil or with clean fill in order to return to the original surface level.

The most extreme of the proposed measures, the sifting protocol is also the only one that can guarantee that all UXO has been removed. However, this method also has significant drawbacks. First, mass excavation of UXO may be unsafe for clearance crews or, at a minimum, may require extreme protective measures. Second, not all soils are amenable to sifting; some are too dense. Third, as discussed later in this monograph, mass excavation of areas destroys the local ecosystem, which is objectionable to some stakeholders, especially at sites with threatened and endangered species.

Table 3.3 illustrates how the controversy over UXO remediation protocols has unfolded at the case study installation described in Chapter Five. (We agreed not to disclose the identity of the installa-

Table 3.3
Comparison of State and DoD Preferences for UXO Cleanup in Areas Slated for Residential Use at a Closed Military Installation

Cleanup Concept	State EPA Perspective	DoD Perspective
Scan existing surface to depth with a metal detector	Required before early transfer [i.e., transfer before cleanup is completed]	Willing where no work has been performed; not willing where DoD has done some surface work
Show that the first five feet of soil contain no UXO, or excavate one foot at a time until the last one-foot lift of soil contains no UXO	Required for residential	Willing to do some of the work, but not all
Scan surface below last clean lift (of one foot of soil)	Required for residential	Not willing
Professional certification that OE (ordnance and explosives) work is done correctly, and written certification of reasonable assurances that no ordnance items are in top five feet	Required for residential	Not willing
Various institutional control and education measures	Required for residential	DoD agrees
On-site, active expert construction support	Required for residential	Willing when UXO is found

SOURCE: Provided by a state environmental regulator working at a closed military installation; the authors agreed not to disclose the identity of the installation in this monograph.

tion because of concerns that doing so would jeopardize ongoing negotiations with UXO remediation contractors.) As shown, the state would like the DoD to guarantee that the first five feet of soil in any area planned for residential development are 100 percent free of UXO. State regulators told us that this would be achieved by following a sifting protocol like that shown in Figure 3.3 to a depth of five feet. The DoD is unwilling to comply with this request.

DoD objects on several grounds to measures, such as the sifting protocol, that go beyond the DDESB guidelines. First, DoD officials contend that the monetary costs are too high. Second, the added protection these options may provide for their extra costs is unclear.

Third, with regard to the sifting protocol, risks to clearance crews from undetected ordnance that may explode during excavation and sifting are unacceptable. And finally, extra excavation in some cases may violate provisions of the Endangered Species Act, because many former ranges contain habitat for threatened and endangered species that would be damaged by disturbing the soil.

All cleanup protocols offer their own advantages and disadvantages. In turn, different vested parties—from local communities, to state regulators, to EPA, to DoD officials—each bring their own priorities into the choice of approach, almost always resulting in conflict. The development of federal guidelines for UXO cleanup (like those for other environmental problems, such as hazardous waste sites and contaminated drinking water supplies) would go a long way toward helping overcome these conflicts, but no such guidelines exist. As a consequence, agreements on UXO clearance processes and end states have not been reached at most BRAC UXO sites.

If past experience is any indicator, the absence of federal standards for UXO remediation means that public health may be compromised. According to GAO (2002b), the Army Corps of Engineers wrongly declared over one-third of former military sites in the FUDS program as clean and in no need of further remediation. GAO determined that the declaration was questionable because there was no evidence available showing that the Corps had obtained and reviewed all the necessary information to identify the hazards at these sites. While the GAO report points out that these findings do not necessarily mean that the sites are in fact contaminated, it cites a number of problems with the way the Corps handled the process of reviewing sites and documenting findings. For instance, the report found that, for 74 percent of all property the Corps designated as "no DoD action indicated" (NDAI), the files failed to make clear that the Corps "reviewed or obtained information such as site maps or photos that would show facilities, such as ammunition storage facilities, that could indicate the presence of hazards (e.g., unexploded ordnance)." The report also estimates that the files for about 60 percent of NDAI properties fail to indicate whether the Corps contacted all the current owners to obtain information about potential hazards. Further, GAO concludes that the Corps appears to have "overlooked or dismissed information in its possession that indicated hazards might be present." In its recommendations, GAO suggests that the Secretary of Defense direct the Corps to develop and implement in a consistent manner more specific guidelines and procedures for assessing FUDS properties (GAO, 2002b).

Regulators, DoD Disagree on Whether CERCLA Applies

In the absence of guidelines specific to UXO remediation, EPA has proposed that all UXO site managers should follow the procedures required for cleanup of hazardous waste sites governed by the Comprehensive Environmental Response, Compensation, and Liability Act (CERCLA), commonly known as Superfund (EPA, 2001). CERCLA regulations cover environmental cleanups from hazardous waste disposal sites and the response to hazardous substance spills, beginning with a preliminary EPA assessment through such steps as hazard ranking, establishment of cleanup goals for the site, design of treatment systems, and system implementation.

Under CERCLA, the EPA must review and approve every step of the cleanup process at a site regulated under this statute. However, CERCLA does not contain provisions specific to UXO. The DoD argues that it, rather than EPA, should have authority over cleanup procedures for military munitions because of the special expertise required to safely excavate and detonate or defuse explosives without injury to workers. For example, in a *Federal Register* notice describing a proposed process for managing UXO sites, the DoD wrote,

> With its years of experience in safely handling and managing UXO, the Department of Defense has the expertise for determining when immediate safety concerns may prevent certain actions to address potential environmental concerns. Due to the specialized mission of the Department of Defense, *the requirement for explosives safety expertise is a critical element unavailable within other organizations* (DoD, 1997, p. 50824, emphasis added).

EPA's Office of Solid Waste and Emergency Response (OSWER), on the other hand, contends that EPA officials should review and sign off on UXO cleanup decisions and that those decisions should be arrived at using the CERCLA process. For example, in a March 2000 letter to the Office of Management and Budget, OSWER's James Woolford contended that "range responses remain subject to CERCLA" (Woolford, 2000).

A guidance document on UXO released jointly by EPA and DoD in 2000 states, "A process consistent with CERCLA . . . will be the preferred response mechanism used to address UXO at a CTT range" (DoD/EPA, 2000). However, the guidance document does not elaborate on what qualifies as a "process consistent with CERCLA." Thus it does little to resolve the disagreements among the agencies.

Conclusion: Disagreement on "How Clean Is Clean" Confounds Cost Estimation

UXO remediation cost estimates are hampered by disagreements as to what constitutes "clean." Technological limitations have driven the EPA and state environmental regulators to suggest cleanup protocols to try to compensate for current detection limitations. However, the lack of federal UXO remediation standards and a regulatory framework for ensuring that those standards are followed has created an environment in which regulators and other vested parties with different agendas promote different and conflicting cleanup protocols.

DoD has generally assumed that cleanup will follow DDESB guidelines, but as this chapter has explained, EPA and state regulators often expect that more extensive UXO searches will be conducted. As Chapter Five will document, the most extensive searches can add as much as hundreds of millions of dollars per installation to the total bill for cleanup. Thus, cost analyses that assume that only DDESB guidelines need to be met may substantially underestimate the total cleanup costs. Different protocols, as will become clear in the coming chapters, lead to vastly different expenditures, further highlighting the uncertainties in cost estimation and the potentially very large range of costs that DoD may need to bear.

CHAPTER FOUR

An Evaluation of the RACER Cost-Estimation Tool

As is clear from the previous chapters, the process of estimating UXO cleanup costs at old military training ranges is fraught with uncertainties. To make decisions about managing these sites, policymakers, regulators, and the military require a reliable cost-estimation tool capable of quantifying costs and associated uncertainties as accurately as possible. As DoD's experience with widely ranging estimates shows (see Chapter Two), a standardized, accurate, and independently validated tool is crucial.

Currently, RACER is the cost-estimation tool most frequently used by the military to estimate the cost of environmental cleanup efforts of all kinds. As part of our study, we conducted a sensitivity analysis of the components of RACER that estimate UXO remediation costs. The purpose was twofold:

1. to evaluate RACER's capabilities—in particular, its usability in calculating the effects of search depth on cost, its sensitivity to variations in other variables and site-specific characteristics, and its ability to be customized to evaluate different UXO cleanup protocol options; and
2. to serve as an initial step toward analyzing the effects of different cleanup protocols—mainly search depth and amount of soil excavation required—on cleanup costs.

This chapter presents the findings of our sensitivity analysis and describes some of the strengths and limitations of RACER.

RACER Is a Standard Tool for Estimating Environmental Cleanup Costs

In 1991, under the supervision of the U.S. Air Force, the consulting firm Earth Tech developed RACER to help the military estimate the costs of various kinds of environmental cleanup. The tool was designed as an easy way to estimate the cost to complete a remediation activity when little or no design information about the cleanup process is available but when a cost estimate is needed for budgeting purposes. Initial versions focused on groundwater and soil contaminants, but in 1997 RACER was expanded for UXO capability with the guidance of the U.S. Army Corps of Engineers (USACE).

RACER is a parametric cost-estimating tool, meaning that it approximates costs based on input parameters specified by the user and/or defaulted by the system. RACER software is available for purchase and operates on any Microsoft Windows system with enough speed and memory to meet the minimum system requirements. Essentially, RACER applies generic engineering solutions to estimate costs, using the historical experience of the environmental remediation industry. The user customizes the generic solution by adding site-specific data to reflect project conditions and requirements. RACER then translates the customized data into quantities of work and produces an estimate using current price data (Earth Tech, 2002).

Overall, RACER is designed to estimate costs based on a minimum amount of data. However, RACER also allows the user to include additional parameters and associated costs in the estimation process by adding user-defined expenses and providing templates to modify the general solution. For instance, the user can modify defaulted labor, equipment, and material assumptions if more specific data are available for the problem at hand. As an example, consider RACER's UXO mapping cost computation screen, shown in Figure 4.1. The screen shows the key cost elements (salaries, equipment purchases and rentals, and so on) that make up the cost of mapping UXO locations. RACER calculates the quantity of each cost element

Figure 4.1
RACER 2002 UXO Mapping Cost Elements Screen

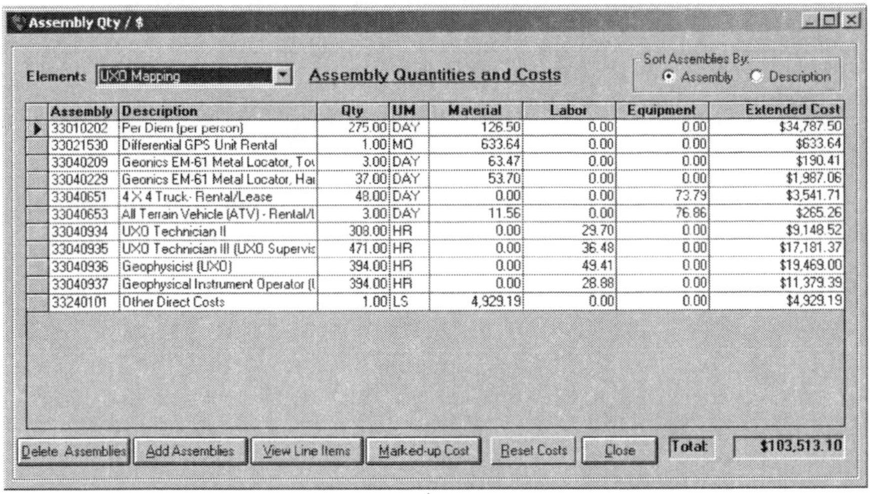
Assembly Qty / $
Elements UXO Mapping
Assembly Quantities and Costs
Sort Assemblies By:
Assembly
Description

Assembly	Description	Qty	UM	Material	Labor	Equipment	Extended Cost
33010202	Per Diem (per person)	275.00	DAY	126.50	0.00	0.00	$34,787.50
33021530	Differential GPS Unit Rental	1.00	MO	633.64	0.00	0.00	$633.64
33040209	Geonics EM-61 Metal Locator, Tov	3.00	DAY	63.47	0.00	0.00	$190.41
33040229	Geonics EM-61 Metal Locator, Har	37.00	DAY	53.70	0.00	0.00	$1,987.06
33040651	4 X 4 Truck- Rental/Lease	48.00	DAY	0.00	0.00	73.79	$3,541.71
33040653	All Terrain Vehicle (ATV) - Rental/l	3.00	DAY	11.56	0.00	76.86	$265.26
33040934	UXO Technician II	308.00	HR	0.00	29.70	0.00	$9,148.52
33040935	UXO Technician III (UXO Supervis	471.00	HR	0.00	36.48	0.00	$17,181.37
33040936	Geophysicist (UXO)	394.00	HR	0.00	49.41	0.00	$19,469.00
33040937	Geophysical Instrument Operator (l	394.00	HR	0.00	28.88	0.00	$11,379.39
33240101	Other Direct Costs	1.00	LS	4,929.19	0.00	0.00	$4,929.19

Delete Assemblies
Add Assemblies
View Line Items
Marked-up Cost
Reset Costs
Close
Total:
$103,513.10

RAND *MG244-4.1*

NOTE: Costs shown are direct costs for the north coast of California. The unit costs shown do not include the contractor's markup. Labor charges are specific to Northern California, which has higher base labor rates than some other locations.

(such as hours of labor required of UXO technicians with different levels of training) based on user-supplied information about the site (acreage, range type, density of ordnance, types of ordnance, and so on). Then, RACER multiplies the estimated quantities by unit costs from a cost database. The cost database reflects average data compiled from construction management agencies, technology contractors and vendors, and historical cost information (PricewaterhouseCoopers, 2001). Costs are specific to location. That is, the user inputs the city and state where the site is located, and RACER adjusts unit costs accordingly. The labor costs shown in Figure 4.1 are for coastal California; they are higher than labor rates in states where the cost of living is lower. The user can override these estimated quantities and unit costs with actual site information (for example, with labor rates specific to the site, if those are known). Also, the user can multiply these costs by markup factors to reflect the additional expenses of overhead, profit, and risk (Earth Tech, 2002). In this report, all costs shown are direct costs, with no markup included.

In its accreditation for RACER 2001, the auditing firm Pricewaterhouse Coopers defines the uses for which the software is validated. It states that RACER is fully accredited

> to provide an automated, consistent and repeatable method to estimate and document the program cost for the environmental cleanup of contaminated sites and to provide a reasonable cost estimate for program funding purposes consistent with the information available at the time of the estimate preparation (PricewaterhouseCoopers, 2001).

This accreditation statement refers to the RACER models and system interface but does not relate to user activities. It also states that RACER models are "designed for a standard generic engineering solution, not for projects that deviate substantially from normal engineering practices" and that RACER is "*completely reliant on user input*, and the reasonableness of the estimate is determined in large part by the *level of site knowledge* the user is able to input into RACER." As these caveats highlight, RACER estimates are only as accurate as the site-specific input information the user provides. Also, modifications in the way RACER is implemented may be needed in order to evaluate remediation protocols that deviate significantly from the standard engineering solution.

The RACER 2001 validation process estimated the accuracy of RACER by analyzing data from 53 remediation projects that have already been completed. However, all of these projects involved conventional contaminants, not UXO. For each project, PricewaterhouseCoopers calculated expected costs according to RACER and then compared these with the reported actual costs. There was an average difference of 3.6 percent between the RACER estimates and the actual costs. No validation specific to the UXO modules has been completed. Similarly, no published comparison of actual costs of UXO cleanup for a specific site versus the costs estimated by RACER was available when we completed this monograph.

Our Analysis Probed RACER's Capacity to Account for UXO Cost Variability

As stated above, the primary purpose of our analysis was to identify (1) how changing RACER's input parameters affects the total cost estimate and (2) which input parameters and assumptions have the most significant influence on cost, as computed by RACER. An ancillary goal was to determine how effective RACER is at accounting for variations in parameters as they relate to cost. Results from this study provide insight as to which UXO removal site characteristics and cleanup processes are more costly and illustrate how each variable assumption can influence labor, equipment, and overall costs. Our analysis also identifies RACER's limitations: potentially important contributors to the total cost that RACER does not consider or does not consider adequately.

Method

For our analysis we used RACER 2002, the most recent version available when we completed this study. Our first step was to identify the appropriate RACER modules to calculate the costs involved in UXO removal actions. RACER includes many different modules for calculating environmental remediation costs, with five modules specific to UXO (described below). Because our focus was on how different UXO search and removal protocols affect costs, we wanted to test only modules containing cost factors related to the search and removal process.

The second step in the analysis was to identify the input variables required by RACER for estimating UXO search and removal costs. We also analyzed whether RACER accounts for all of the variables that could be important in estimating costs of UXO remediation.

The third step of the study consisted of testing RACER's sensitivity to the different input variables. We varied the values of the critical inputs one at a time, holding everything else constant. This step was intended to identify RACER's sensitivity to each variable.

We also tested the dependencies of one variable on another, holding everything else constant.

The fourth step involved the identification and analysis of the parameters that have the largest influence on the overall cost of a UXO cleanup effort. These results help reveal which UXO site characteristics and removal processes are most costly, according to RACER.

Step 1: Identify RACER Module for Analysis

As noted above, RACER contains five modules specifically designed for estimating costs associated with UXO response. These modules are based on historical data from the USACE Huntsville Engineering Center (Peterson and Peterson, 2001). They correspond to the budget phases of planning for management and cleanup of UXO at closed, transferred, and transferring ranges. The five modules are:

1. **Archives Search Report.** Calculates the cost of identifying locations within an installation that may contain UXO, based on reviews of historical documents and interviews with former military personnel.

2. **OE Site Characterization and Removal Assessment.** Calculates the cost of characterizing the nature and estimated quantity of ordnance mainly by studying a sample area of the site.

3. **OE Removal Action.** Includes the cost of searching for, marking, removing, and destroying UXO.

4. **OE Monitoring.** Determines the cost of site monitoring following UXO removal, in case any ordnance was left behind. (According to USACE, at least one review every 5 years is needed to ensure public safety.)

5. **OE Institutional Controls.** Includes the cost of educational programs, deed restrictions, fences, signs, and other mechanisms to prevent civilian injuries from UXO remaining on site.

Our sensitivity analysis focuses on the OE Removal Action Module, which calculates the costs for mapping the locations of and removing UXO. This module accounts for the most significant part of remediation costs and includes the key cost factors that would change when search and removal protocols are varied. As Figure 4.2 shows, the OE Removal Action Module sorts the total costs into six categories: site visit, vegetation removal, UXO mapping, UXO removal/detonation, site management, and stakeholder involvement.

Step 2: Identify Input Parameters

The OE Removal Action Module requires the user to specify a large number of input variables providing details about the site. Table 4.1 shows a number of the key input variables and their definitions. For our analysis, we formulated a fictional site and assessed the sensitivity of the cost estimate to changes in these variables. The third column of Table 4.1 shows our assumed input values for the fictional site. During our sensitivity analysis, we held all variables to these constant levels except the one or two we were analyzing. All variables not specified in Table 4.1 were held to RACER default values.[1]

In reviewing the required input variables, we noticed that the OE Removal Action Module does not account for two site characteristics that could affect overall costs: soil type and duration of range use.

Figure 4.2
RACER UXO Modules and Removal Cost Classifications

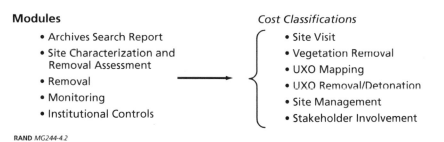

Modules

- Archives Search Report
- Site Characterization and Removal Assessment
- Removal
- Monitoring
- Institutional Controls

Cost Classifications

- Site Visit
- Vegetation Removal
- UXO Mapping
- UXO Removal/Detonation
- Site Management
- Stakeholder Involvement

RAND MG244-4.2

---

[1] Our analysis did not test all possible input variables.

Table 4.1
Input Variables in RACER 2002's OE Removal Action Module

Required Input Variable	Meaning	Assumed Value for Sensitivity Analysis
Removal area	Acreage to be cleared	9,000 acres
Vegetation	Types of plants present	Low grass and few shrubs
Search depth	Depth to which clearance crews will search for UXO	5 feet
Topography	Steepness of terrain	Gently rolling
Worker per diem	Subsistence expenses provided to personnel from off-site locations	Excluded; assumed all personnel were on site
Ordnance type	Types of ordnance found at the site	High-explosive bombs
Percentage scrap	Percentage of detected anomalies that are scrap (nonexplosive) items	90% (RACER default)
Density (range type)	Historical use of the range (used by RACER to assign density value: i.e., number of UXO and non-UXO metal items per acre)	Multiple use (trial 1); bombing range (trial 2)
UXO mapping method	Whether anomaly locations are recorded in a global positioning system database, or only with flags	Conventional (flags)
Mag-and-flag teams	Number of crews involved in searching for UXO	3
Ordnance locator	Type of metal detector used	Schonstedt model GA-72CV (hand-held magnetometer)
Surface clearance teams	Number of crews involved in clearing surface UXO	3
Ordnance destruction method	Method for detonating any live ordnance found	30% electrical; 70% in-grid consolidation (RACER defaults)
Ordnance destruction teams	Number of teams involved in detonating UXO	3
Level of detail required for UXO removal report	Amount of effort required to prepare UXO removal report	Moderate (RACER default)
Stakeholder involvement	Degree to which stakeholders will be consulted	Moderate (RACER default)

Table 4.1 (continued)

Required Input Variable	Meaning	Assumed Value for Sensitivity Analysis
Community meetings	Number of formal meetings with the local community	2 (RACER default)
Required additional reports (other than UXO removal report)	Formal written reports required (work plan, explosives safety submission, both)	Work plan and explosives safety submission (RACER default)

Soil type, such as clay, gravel, rock, silt, and sand, could affect the level of effort required to excavate buried ordnance. In fact, USACE research identified soil type as one of the key cost drivers of the ordnance search and removal effort (Crull, Taylor, and Tipton, 1999). As an example, if humans are completing the excavation effort using shovels and other manual tools, soil type may have a significant impact on human performance rate because some soil types are more difficult to shovel than others. U.S. Army Corps of Engineers regulations require that all excavation within 12 inches of a UXO item be performed manually. RACER does not account for differences in the manual labor required for different soil types. Further, different soil types may require different treatment for the excavation process, especially for deep excavations. For example, Occupational Safety and Health Administration (OSHA) standards for excavation define specific sloping requirements depending on the soil type. Soil type also affects the performance of UXO detection technologies. For example, metal detectors perform very poorly on high-iron soil. Furthermore, the penetration depth of the ordnance depends on the soil type, along with ordnance characteristics (Crull, Taylor, and Tipton, 1999), so soil type affects the expected anomaly density at different search depths. By not including soil type, RACER's OE Removal Action Module fails to account for these factors.[2]

---

[2] Although it is not a parameter included in the RACER 2002 UXO Removal Action Module, RACER training materials provided to us indicate that soil type was once included in

The length of time the range was in use also could affect cost, due to the potential effect on the density of ordnance and scrap, and RACER does not account for this either. For example, a range used for military training purposes for a half century could be expected to have more ordnance and scrap than a site with the same characteristics but used for only a few years. The number of times the site was scanned for ordnance while still an active range also might be a factor in estimating density. RACER, however, does not account for this factor. The user's only way to compensate is to determine manually the effects of range-use duration on density and then replace RACER's default density values with these new inputs.

Step 3: Analyze Module Sensitivity to Input Variables

We analyzed RACER's sensitivity to variations in each variable listed in Table 4.1. First, we tested variations in the physical characteristics of the site (removal area, topography, vegetation removal, anomaly density, ordnance type, percentage scrap). Then, we analyzed cleanup characteristics (clearance depth, surveying methods, UXO mapping techniques, and the number of cleanup teams).

Removal Area. As expected, RACER shows a direct association between cost and the total acreage of land targeted for cleanup efforts. As Figure 4.3 illustrates, as acreage increases, total costs rise, as one would expect. As shown in Figure 4.4, there is a significant economy of scale: costs per acre decrease as total acreage increases.

Topography. Within RACER, topography, such as whether the range is flat, gently rolling, or contains gorges or gullies, has an impact on the rate of search and, as a result, on the overall project duration. Project duration in turn affects costs. As Figure 4.5 shows, RACER calculates the costs of cleaning flat terrain at about 30 percent less than the costs of clearing mountainous terrain for a density of 50 items per acre and about 20 percent less for a density of 400 items per acre.

RACER but (for reasons that were not disclosed to us) was removed in the later version of the software.

Figure 4.3
Effect of Size of UXO Removal Area on Total Cost

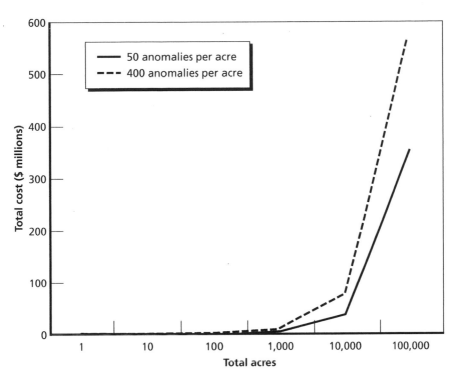

RAND MG244-4.3

Vegetation Removal. As discussed in Chapter Three, removing vegetation is generally the first step in any UXO remediation. To calculate associated costs, RACER assigns percentages of the total acreage to each of four levels of vegetation removal effort: no removal, light removal, moderate removal, and heavy removal. The amount of acreage assigned to each category depends on the type of vegetation the user selects: barren or low grass, low grass and few shrubs, heavy grass with numerous shrubs, shrubs with some trees, or heavy shrubs with trees. As Figure 4.6 shows, RACER estimates that total cleanup costs are significantly less for barren land than for sites with heavy shrubbery, as one would expect. Heavily vegetated sites are approximately twice as costly to clear as barren or grassy areas.

Figure 4.4
Effect of Size of UXO Removal Area on Per-Acre Cost

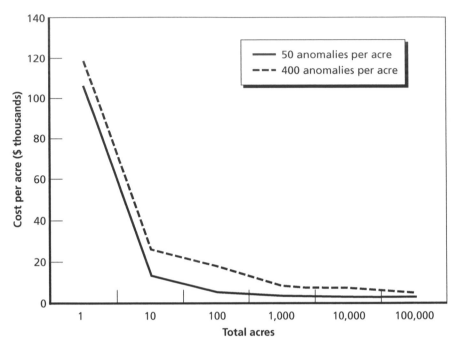

Decisions as to which vegetation removal method to use—manual, controlled burning, or defoliation—are generally based on the amount of vegetation that needs to be removed, the feasibility of use under specific site conditions, and the environmental effects of the method. RACER provides no capability for designating the vegetation removal method to be used, although it may be an important cost factor when combined with other site-specific characteristics. Take for example the potential effect of topography on vegetation removal. If mechanized methods are used to aid the operation, topography may limit the site's accessibility and the machine's performance, thus increasing the time to complete the operation (likewise for manual operations, in which human performance and the speed of the operation may be somewhat reduced on mountainous sites). On

Figure 4.5
Effect of Topography on Total Cost

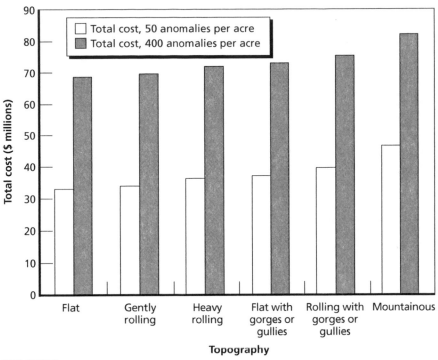

the other hand, if controlled fire is used for vegetation removal, then topography may not have a significant effect on the cost.

Anomaly Density. RACER's help manuals define anomaly density as the total number of UXO plus scrap items per acre. Density is a critical variable to determine cost because the number of anomalies directly affects the excavation time. Rather than requiring the user to input density values, RACER assigns a default density based on the range type (see Table 4.2). The user can overwrite the default density values, if the actual densities are known.

Figure 4.7 shows that, as expected, cleanup costs estimated by RACER increase linearly with density. For example, the cost more than doubles in our sensitivity analysis for range types with density

Figure 4.6
Effect of Vegetation on Cost

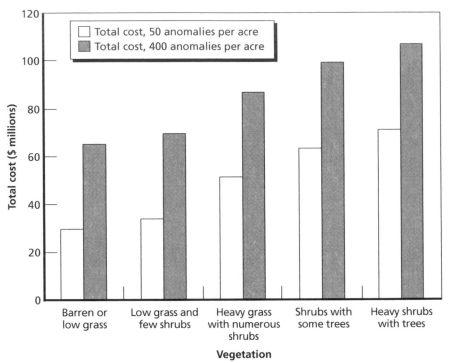

values of 400 (the maximum possible density in RACER) as compared to those with density values of 50. The total cost increases by $5.1 million for every increase in density of 50 items per acre (when using inputs as identified in Table 4.1).

In practice, density may vary depending on how long the property was used for ordnance training and testing and how often ordnance and scrap were picked up while the site was in use. However, as noted earlier, RACER does not provide the capability to consider the time-length of use, or how often the site was cleared.

In theory, density should also depend on two other factors: ordnance type and search depth (the depth to which the search for ordnance is conducted). Some bombs, missiles, and rockets can penetrate

Figure 4.7
Effect of Anomaly Density on Cost

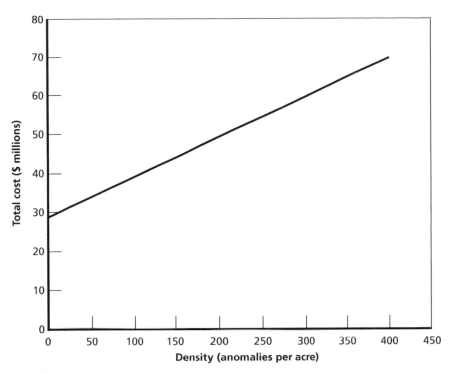

to great depths, while other ordnance (such as mines and grenades) is often found at surface or near-surface levels, depending on factors such as angle of entry and ordnance weight (DoD, 2001a). Many factors influence the depth at which the ordnance will be found, including munitions size, shape, and soil characteristics.

To investigate the effect of ordnance type and search depth on density and cost as computed by RACER, we performed the following three tests:

- We varied the search depths while holding range type constant. We found that RACER defaulted to the density assigned to the specific range type, regardless of the search depth specified.

Table 4.2
RACER Default Values for Anomaly Density, Based on Range Type

Range Type	Default Density (Total Anomalies per Acre)
Air-to-air	50
Air-to-ground	300
Artillery	200
Bombing	50
Guided missile	50
Burial pit	1
Hand grenade	50
Open burn/open detonation	300
Mortar	250
Multiple/combined use	400
Rifle grenade, anti-tank rocket	150
Small arms	250

- We varied ordnance type while holding range type constant. We found that RACER defaulted to the density assigned to the specific range type, regardless of ordnance type specified.
- We varied search depth, range type, and ordnance type simultaneously. We found that RACER defaulted to the density assigned to each specific range type, regardless of the combination of search depth and ordnance type specified.

As is evident, RACER cannot account for the influence of either ordnance type or search depth on anomaly density and instead relies on default densities. Given the real-world impact both have on the density of items excavated, this gap represents a significant limitation.

Ordnance Type. As the density tests show, ordnance type, despite its impact on density and thus cost, appears to have no role in RACER calculations. Indeed, the tool exhibited no change in cost based on the ordnance type specified. We ran additional tests to determine if RACER recognizes relationships between the range type and the ordnance type and the ordnance type and cost required for detonation. There was no cost difference in either case. Thus, although ordnance type is a RACER input, it appears to have no effect on cost.

Percentage Scrap. Within RACER, percentage scrap is defined as the percentage of anomalies identified by the metal detector that are not intact UXO items. RACER assumes that the percentage scrap affects the cost of ordnance detonation, but not the cost of excavating the item, since all identified anomalies must be recovered before determining if they are scrap or not.

As Figure 4.8 shows, cost decreases linearly with the percentage of scrap. The decrease is steeper for a density of 400 than for a density of 50 anomalies per acre. The cost decrease results from having

Figure 4.8
Effect of Percentage Scrap on Cost

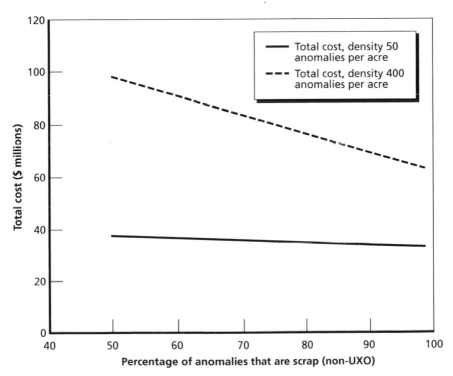

fewer ordnance items to detonate when a greater number of anomalies are scrap items rather than UXO.

Clearance Depth. RACER allows for cost variations with depth only in three depth categories: greater than zero to less than three feet, three feet to less than five feet, and five feet to less than ten feet. In other words, within each of these depth ranges, it holds the cost factors constant, meaning RACER assumes that the costs of clearance to two feet are the same as those to one foot, costs for clearance to three feet are the same as those for four feet, and so on. For depths of three feet or more, RACER increases the total man-hours required to remove anomalies by 15 percent. For depths of five feet or more, RACER increases the number of backhoes used for excavation. These increases in man-hours and number of backhoes, however, have very little effect on cost as computed by RACER. Figure 4.9 shows that the cost is nearly constant with clearance depth.

In reality, increasing the search depth could increase costs more than RACER is able to reflect. Increasing the clearance depth requires digging and moving more dirt, which is a costly process. Further, additional, costly engineering and safety measures might be needed for deep excavations. For instance, for excavations of five feet or greater, OSHA requires safeguards to protect workers from potential cave-ins of material that can fall or roll into an excavation. In general, OSHA requires that in all excavations employees must be protected by sloping or benching the sides of the excavation, supporting the sides of the excavation, or placing a shield between the side of the excavation and the work area (OSHA-1926.651[j]). The materials and effort involved in emplacing protective equipment can affect both the cost of the operation and the time to completion. RACER does not account for these potential costs.

Moreover, RACER works under the assumption that backhoes will always be used for completing excavations, even when an excavation is only one foot deep. USACE documentation on OE removal, however, establishes that anomalies deeper than one foot may be excavated using either mechanical or manual methods (U.S. Army Corps of Engineers, 2000). However, USACE also prohibits the use

Figure 4.9
Effect of Clearance Depth on Cost

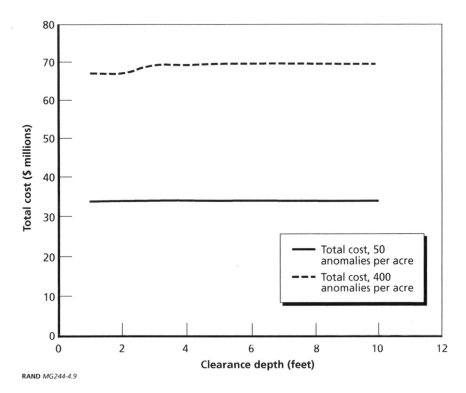

of earth-moving machinery (including backhoes) within 12 inches of a suspected UXO item (U.S. Army Corps of Engineers, 2001). As a result, some manual excavation is always required, but RACER does not appear to account for this. It is likely that the performance and length of the operation will vary depending on the method used. That is, if excavation is primarily performed manually by humans with shovels and picks, the effort involved in deeper excavations would be much greater, considering human performance factors, the multiple scanning effort involved in searching greater depths, and the fact that the hole needs to have a larger diameter to be able to hold such depth without collapsing. Unfortunately, because it only accounts for backhoes, RACER cannot accommodate these distinctions.

All told, one would expect search depth to significantly influence cleanup cost. Certainly, DoD and EPA officials involved in overseeing UXO remediation perceive that depth is a significant cost factor. For example, EPA's handbook for UXO site managers states, "The depth at which OE is located is a primary determinant of both potential human exposure and the cost of the investigation and cleanup" (EPA, 2001). Indeed, one of the primary arguments from the military during negotiations about UXO remediation requirements is that clearing UXO to depths of more than one or two feet is too costly. That RACER cannot account for cost variations with clearance depth is a significant limitation.

Other Cleanup Variables. Several other variables also affect RACER cost estimation. We tested RACER sensitivity to some but not all of these. Examples include the following:

Number of Teams. As might be expected, the greater the number of mag-and-flag teams, surface clearance teams, and ordnance destruction teams, the lower the cost (because of the decreased time and overhead required to complete the operation). For example, costs decreased by 25 percent when our sensitivity analysis assumed that eight teams instead of one were deployed (for a density of 50 items per acre).

Ordnance Locator Type. The choice of ordnance locator mechanism (i.e., metal detector brand) affects cost due mostly to the equipment rental charges rather than to the cost associated with the detection capability or false alarm rate. Overall, changing the detector type affected costs by at most about 2 percent in our sensitivity analysis. As discussed in Chapter Three, different types of detection equipment have different false alarm rates. False alarm rates can significantly affect cost by making the UXO remediation effort slower when many false alarms need to be excavated. To account for variations in false alarm rates among different detectors, the user would need to override the default value for percentage scrap; RACER does not make this change automatically when the detector type is changed. Instead, RACER assumes that all detectors have equal false alarm rates.

Community Involvement and Reporting Requirements. RACER also includes as input factors the number of community meetings required, the amount of stakeholder involvement, the level of detail of the final UXO removal report, and the number and types of additional reports (work plans and so on) required. However, none of these factors had a large influence on cost in our sensitivity analysis. Intuitively, some of the factors may be more significant than RACER reflects. For example, although RACER computes a slight decrease in costs where stakeholder involvement is low, decreasing the amount of stakeholder involvement may actually increase costs when the potential consequences—such as lawsuits caused by disagreements after the cleanup is completed—are considered.

Site Management and Quality Assurance Requirements. RACER allows the user to modify its assumptions about how many total hours will be required of site managers and of quality assurance personnel (those who recheck portions of cleared areas after the crews have finished their initial round of work). We did not alter RACER's calculations of time requirements for these personnel. Presumably, though, increasing the hours required of quality assurance and other site management personnel will increase costs accordingly.

Step 4: Analyze Major Influences on Cost

We used the results of the sensitivity analysis to identify the factors of the cleanup effort that RACER indicates as having the largest impact on cost. Table 4.3 presents the maximum cost differences associated with each variable, using the input variables shown in Table 4.1. The cost differences seen reflect the change in total cost that occurs when the input variable is adjusted from its minimum possible value to its maximum possible value (as seen in the second column of the table).

As is evident from Table 4.3,

- The variables with the most significant influence on RACER's output are total acreage, anomaly density, and vegetation.
- Clearance depth is not a critical parameter according to RACER. The minimal cost effects within RACER, however,

Table 4.3
Maximum Cost Difference for Critical Variables

Variable	Parameter Range	Maximum Cost Difference, $ millions (density = 400 anomalies per acre)	Maximum Cost Difference, $ millions (density = 50 anomalies per acre)
Total acreage	1 to 100,000 acres	570.8	349.6
Vegetation removal	Barren to heavy	41.4	41.4
Number of ordnance destruction teams	1 to 8 teams	40.7	5.1
Percentage scrap	50% to 99%	35.0	4.4
Topography	Flat to mountainous	13.5	13.5
Number of mag-and-flag teams	1 to 8 teams	8.8	8.8
Clearance depth	1 to 10 feet	2.3	0.3
Number of surface clearance teams	1 to 8 teams	1.1	1.1

conflict with the DoD and EPA view of depth as a primary determinant in the cost of UXO remediation (EPA, 2001).

- For sites with a high density of UXO, the number of ordnance destruction teams and percentage scrap are also important cost drivers.
- For both categories of sites, additional cost drivers are topography and the number of mag-and-flag teams.

Conclusion: RACER Has Strengths, but Accuracy Could Be Improved

RACER has a number of positive attributes. It accounts for most of the key variables that influence UXO remediation costs. It allows users to easily override default values and thus is flexible in the amount of data required to operate it. It also is easy to learn and use. However, our sensitivity analysis also illustrates some important limitations, including the following:

- **Clearance depth.** RACER estimates that the cost involved in removing ordnance is nearly constant with search depth. However, both DoD and EPA have suggested that depth is a critical parameter in cost estimates. RACER does not appear to adequately account for the effect of clearance depth on cost.
- **Soil type.** RACER does not consider cost differences related to the effort involved in removing ordnance from different soil types, such as clay, gravel, rock, sand, and ferrous. Additionally, RACER does not account for the ways that anomaly density is modified through different depths based on the soil type.
- **Backhoe usage.** RACER assumes the use of backhoes on any excavation operation. If no backhoes are employed, users can remove the cost to rent or lease the default backhoes. RACER, however, makes no adjustments for the difference in the effort involved (human performance) in removing ordnance with or without backhoes. Users thus need to make additional manual adjustments to account for the lack of backhoes.
- **Vegetation removal.** The effort involved in removing vegetation is assumed to be the same regardless of the topography of the terrain. Costs estimated for removing vegetation on flat land are the same as those estimated for removing vegetation from mountainous areas. There is no capability to specify if the vegetation removal will be performed with fire, with machinery, or manually by humans.
- **Anomaly density.** RACER does not estimate density based on the length of time a range was used for a specific purpose; instead, it defaults to a constant density based on the range type and size. Further, RACER does not account for the fact that range use can change over time. These default density values can, however, be overwritten.

.

CHAPTER FIVE

Case Study: Effect of UXO Clearance Requirements on Cost

As Chapter Three explained, no national consensus has emerged on how to render land contaminated with UXO safe for nonmilitary reuse. A number of different approaches have been suggested, from clearing only UXO visible on the ground surface, to searching with metal detectors and digging up all metal items found up to a specified depth, to excavating all the contaminated soil. In this chapter, we analyze the cost implications of different approaches to UXO clearance at an actual DoD installation. We calculate three sets of cost estimates for this installation in order to illustrate the budgetary implications of three different cleanup protocols: one preferred by the military, the second preferred by the state environmental regulators, and a third that could serve as a compromise. To generate the estimates, we manually adjusted some of RACER's computations to account for factors such as variations in UXO density with depth and soil excavation effort. The results of our work highlight that varying assumptions about end states for UXO cleanup (i.e., what constitutes a "clean" site) can have a major impact on cost estimates.

To estimate the costs of the three different UXO remediation alternatives, we proceeded as follows:

1. **Site selection.** Based primarily on data availability, we chose a site to serve as the basis for our case study cost estimates.

2. **Cleanup protocol identification.** First, we identified two conflicting cleanup protocols. Both have been proposed as clearance strategies for the case study installation. We identified a third

protocol that could serve as a compromise approach. The protocols involve varying the depths to which UXO is cleared, the amounts of soil excavated, and the number of repeat searches with a metal detector, as explained later in this chapter.

3. **Cost estimations for cleanup protocols.** The standard method for implementing RACER does not adequately account for the effects of clearance depth, extra soil excavation, or repeat searches with a metal detector on cost. However, we were able to manually adjust RACER's computations to account for changes in these factors. We used RACER and actual site data provided by the case study installation to estimate the costs of each of the three cleanup protocols.

Site Was Chosen Based on Data Availability

Critical to our analysis was the ability to obtain site-specific information to match the central parameters required by RACER. Consequently, we based our choice primarily on the site offering the greatest availability of data: a former multi-use range that had been closed under BRAC and whose ongoing cleanup translated into a large amount of existing data. For confidentiality reasons, the name of the installation will not be disclosed in this report.[1] Instead, we will refer to it as Site A.

Although cleanup at Site A has been ongoing for years, the military and the state have been unable to agree on a UXO clearance protocol sufficient to protect the public. Such conflicts are common at BRAC UXO sites. For example, a RAND Arroyo Center analysis of Army BRAC sites found that the Army has been able to complete the cleanup and transfer of only about 10 percent of Army BRAC acreage with UXO, due in part to disagreements about the cleanup process (MacDonald, Knopman, et al., 2005). Exacerbating the efforts to

---

[1] Installation officials requested that we keep the name, location, and service affiliation of the installation confidential because they were in the process of obtaining bids from UXO clearance contractors and did not want our research to bias the bidding process.

reach an agreement are environmental concerns. Site A is home to endangered vegetation, and certain cleanup protocols would damage the natural habitat. Further, a community resides close to Site A. Incidents have been recorded of civilians coming in contact with UXO, increasing the public's concerns about the success of the remediation process.

Because cleanup efforts at the site have been under way for a long time, complete data were available on the density of UXO in different site sectors, percentage of scrap (as compared to UXO), variation in UXO density with depth, planned remediation technologies, vegetation, and topography. Our ongoing relationship with site officials facilitated the communication process and made the data readily available to us. Table 5.1 documents the data we requested and obtained from these officials.

Table 5.1
Data Requested from Case Study Site

Information Requested	Information Obtained
Total acreage for remediation	Approximately 7,000 acres
Grid divisions	Map of the UXO-affected area, showing approximately two dozen grids into which the site has been divided for remediation purposes, and acreage of each grid
Planned technologies	Metal detection technologies planned for use on each grid
Soil type	Sand
Vegetation	Vegetation types specific to each grid
Topography	Topography specific to each grid
UXO density	Estimated density specific to each grid
Vertical density distribution	Variation in UXO density with depth for the entire site up to four feet of depth, based on actual data
Percentage scrap	Amount of metal scrap as a percentage of total anomalies found with metal detectors, based on actual data

Site A occupies about 7,000 acres of contaminated land targeted for UXO remediation. The total acreage was divided into about two dozen grids following standard UXO cleanup procedures. Site officials provided us with a map detailing the grid sizes and locations along with a spreadsheet containing pertinent data for each section of the grid.

Site A officials also provided data showing the vertical distribution of all the UXO items retrieved to date. Table 5.2 shows this distribution. As one would expect, most (72 percent) of the UXO is buried in the first foot of soil, and no significant amounts have been found below four feet of depth. This is not necessarily true at other sites; as Chapter Three explained, sometimes ordnance can be found at much greater depths.

In addition to the density distribution with depth, we obtained percentage scrap values for the site. Unfortunately, the values provided for individual sectors were not useful for RACER data input due to conflicting definitions. For Site A officials, percentage scrap is the number of UXO scrap items (i.e., shrapnel and other debris from munitions) found versus the number of whole UXO items found, without considering non-UXO-related scrap (such as parts of corroded vehicles, soup cans, and coins) that were also excavated. RACER, in contrast, defines percentage scrap as the total number of excavated scrap (nonhazardous) items, including those originating from ordnance and those from other sources.

Table 5.2
Variation in UXO Density with Depth at Site A

Depth Interval	Percentage of Total UXO Items Found in Depth Interval
Surface	21%
≤ 1 foot	72%
> 1 foot to ≤ 2 feet	5%
> 2 feet to ≤ 3 feet	1%
> 3 feet to ≤ 4 feet	1%

To account for this discrepancy, instead of using the percentage scrap values provided for each grid, we used sitewide data on the total number of items excavated and the number of these that were non-hazardous, versus UXO, items. In total, site officials told us, 5,500,000 items located by metal detectors have been excavated and examined. Of these, 49,000, or about 1 percent of the total, were whole UXO. So, we used a percent scrap value of 99 percent for all the grids. Notably, this is also the value that DoD reported as "typical" in the preliminary cost estimate to Congress described in Chapter Two.

Cleanup Protocols Conflict

As discussed in Chapter Three, federal and state regulatory agencies routinely debate the best protocol to achieve cleanup goals. At Site A, the various groups involved in decisionmaking (military, state, EPA, and local governments) have suggested several very different protocols. We chose two of the protocols for our analysis, plus a third that represents a compromise. They are summarized in Table 5.3. The military prefers protocol 1, and the state has contended that protocol

Table 5.3
UXO Clearance Protocols Considered in Our Analysis

Protocol 1 (Military)	Protocol 2 (State)	Protocol 3 (Compromise)
• Scan entire site once using best available metal detectors • Dig all anomalies found • Provide construction support to property developers in case any UXO is discovered during construction	• Excavate entire site in one-foot depth increments, scanning with a metal detector before each excavation • Sift the excavated soil • Backfill with sifted or clean soil	• Scan entire site once using best available metal detectors • Dig all anomalies found • Repeat one or more times for entire area or portions of it

2 should guide the cleanup at least in areas slated for residential development. Protocol 3 is an alternative that could be considered for increasing the probability of finding UXO without completely excavating the site, as required under protocol 2.

Results from our RACER sensitivity analysis (Chapter Four) identified the tool's critical cost-estimation parameters as well as its limitations. With these limitations in mind, we customized the RACER implementation method to simulate the three cleanup protocols for Site A and estimate the cost differences among them.

Cleanup Protocol 1

The first cleanup protocol (see Figure 5.1) is relatively straightforward and is the conventional approach generally advocated by the military. It consists of scanning the land once with the best available metal detection technology, then excavating and removing all the anomalies that are identified up to a specified depth, and finally agreeing to remove any residual UXO that is found after the land has been transferred.

The principal challenge of this protocol is ensuring the detection of the majority of UXO. As Chapter Three explained, metal detectors are less than 100 percent effective in finding UXO, and this approach inevitably will leave behind some UXO. This results in a potential safety hazard for future land development workers, who may not be trained to address UXO risks and did not sign up for UXO remediation work as part of the development project. Further, safety concerns may remain for area residents, who may mistakenly believe that the land is clean since remediation was mandated before transfer.

Figure 5.1
Cleanup Protocol 1

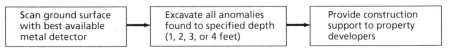

| Scan ground surface with best available metal detector | → | Excavate all anomalies found to specified depth (1, 2, 3, or 4 feet) | → | Provide construction support to property developers |

In calculating the costs of this protocol, we made two adjustments to the standard method for computing costs with RACER. First, after learning from Site A officials that backhoes are used less frequently than RACER assumes, we manually removed the cost of backhoe rental when estimating the cost of surface clearance and clearance to depths of up to two feet. Second, we used the vertical density distribution provided by Site A officials to calculate the variation in density with depth, rather than relying on RACER's assumption that UXO is evenly distributed with depth. We assumed that only the anomalies present at less than or equal to the specified depth would be excavated, and that any deeper anomalies would be left behind. As an example, if the excavation goal was one foot and a metal detector signaled an anomaly, the excavation would stop at one foot, even if the anomaly were not found.

Cleanup Protocol 2

The second cleanup protocol is equivalent to the "sifting method" described in Chapter Three and illustrated in Figure 3.3 (page 23). As discussed in Chapter Three, the sifting method involves surveying the site for UXO, excavating all the soil, and sifting it in one-foot depth increments. The sifting method is the only protocol that ensures the removal of UXO up to a specific maximum depth. The approach, however, raises cost and environmental concerns. The military has contended that the costs associated with this approach may be excessive. Scanning and excavation are the two primary sources of cost for UXO remediation activities. The cost of removing entire layers of soil and rescanning the land at the new surface levels is considerable and may not be economically feasible or justified by the potential economic gain of developing the land. The sifting method also permanently destroys the vegetation and soil structure of the site. This environmental impact is a major concern for the clearance of Site A, because it hosts endangered vegetation that has, paradoxically, been preserved on the site due to development restrictions imposed by its UXO threat.

The sifting method varies considerably from the standard UXO remediation approach that RACER assumes. The main challenge in developing cost estimates for this alternative is to develop a RACER implementation strategy that can reproduce the approach.

The two most outstanding differences between this method and protocol 1 are the involvement of multiple scanning efforts at each foot of depth, after the overlying soil has been excavated, and the effort required to remove all the soil, instead of only digging small holes to recover metal objects located by the metal detector. We accounted for these differences by altering the standard process for implementing the RACER OE Removal Action Module in three ways:

1. As with protocol 1, we used the vertical density distribution provided by site officials to calculate the expected densities at surface, one-, two-, three-, and four-foot depth increments. For protocol 2, however, since UXO removal excavations would be performed in one-foot increments, we used the density contained in each one-foot soil layer, rather than the cumulative density. That is, if the total anomaly density per acre was 100, we assumed 93 items would be found per acre on the surface and in the first foot of soil, 5 items would be found between one and two feet, and one item each would be found between two and three feet and between three and four feet, based on the data shown in Table 5.2.

2. We ran the OE Removal Action Module several times to simulate multiple scanning efforts. For every grid, we ran this module once using density values for the first foot of soil, a second time using densities for the layer between one and two feet, and so on down to four feet. We counted the costs for site preparation and reporting, vegetation removal, and stakeholder involvement only once for each grid, since these costs would not have to be incurred again with each additional layer of soil removed.

3. We used RACER's Excavation Module (which is separate from the OE Removal Action Module) to estimate excavation costs. We used this module to estimate the cost of removing one-foot layers of soil in between UXO scanning efforts. It is important to note, however, that the general excavation module was not

created for UXO projects. As a result, the costs resulting from this module represent a site with similar characteristics, such as soil type and acreage, but without any UXO safety considerations. The main input parameters required for the RACER Excavation Module are soil type and total acreage.

Cleanup Protocol 3

The third cleanup protocol can be viewed as a compromise between the first two. It involves completing protocol 1 once, and then repeating the entire process one or more times to locate any UXO and other anomalies missed on the first scan, as illustrated in Figure 5.2. Repeat scanning with a metal detector should, in theory, substantially increase the probability of detecting UXO items, especially those buried at depths of less than two feet. With each scan, the amount of metal scrap will decrease, and thus the detector can be fine-tuned to look for UXO.

At Site A, two primary kinds of metal detectors are used: a device known as an EM 61 (which automatically records the location of each find on a global positioning system) and a second device known as a Schoenstedt 72CV (used for conventional mag-and-flag surveys). Extensive field trials at Site A showed that the average probability of detecting UXO or UXO-related scrap was 60 percent for the EM 61 and 76 percent for the Schoenstedt. Based on these data, to achieve a probability of detection of near 100 percent without excavation

Figure 5.2
Cleanup Protocol 3

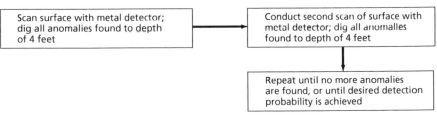

would require multiple scans of the site to pick up items missed on the initial scan. For example, for the Schoenstedt device, the first scan would find 76 percent of the UXO. A second scan would at most find 76 percent of the remaining 24 percent of UXO items, for a total detection rate of 94 percent. Table 5.4 shows how the probability of finding UXO should, theoretically, increase for each additional scan for the two detectors. It is critical to note, however, that the assumption that subsequent scans would detect UXO not found the first time is only theoretical. The actual performance of detectors in finding items missed on the first scan would need to be determined in field tests. Some UXO items might remain undetected despite multiple scans, due to their depth, orientation, and size. The metal content of the soil could also influence the effectiveness of repeat scans.

To simulate the costs of this protocol, we ran the RACER OE Removal Action Module multiple times to reflect the additional scanning effort. Site A officials provided us with data on the amount of acreage within each grid to be surveyed with the different detectors. So, if an area was scanned with an EM 61 and the anomaly density of the area was 100 items per acre, then the first scan would locate 60 items and leave a density of 40 items per acre to be searched during the second scan, and so on. We assumed a search depth of

Table 5.4
Theoretical Best-Case Effect of Number of Scans on
Probability That a UXO Item Will Be Found at Site A

Number of Scans	Detector	
	EM 61	Schoenstedt 72CV
1	60%	76%
2	84%	94%
3	94%	99%
4	97%	100%
5	100%	—

four feet for each run. As with protocol 2, we counted site-preparation and reporting costs only once.

We Estimated the Costs of the Three Protocols

Using the methods described above, we calculated the direct (i.e., not marked up) UXO remediation costs for all three protocols (and for several variations of the first two using different maximum clearance depths). For all the calculations, we computed the cost for each individual grid using the data provided by Site A. Actual costs would be higher due to markups from contractors to account for overhead, profits, and risk.

Figure 5.3 shows the results for protocol 1 (the standard UXO response process) carried out to different depths. As shown, the cost

Figure 5.3
Direct Costs of Clearing UXO According to Protocol 1, Implemented to Different Depths

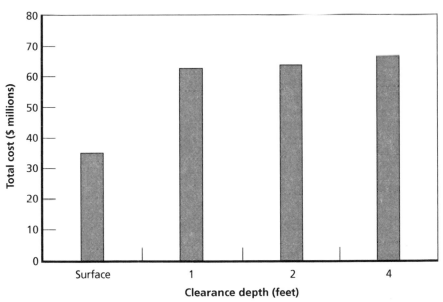

of any UXO clearance to below-surface depths is nearly double the cost of surface clearance alone, but the costs of clearing to a depth of four feet are only about 6 percent more than the costs of clearing to one foot according to protocol 1. Most likely, this is because 93 percent of the ordnance is found on the surface and in the first foot of soil. Sites with higher concentrations of deep ordnance probably would not exhibit the same result.

Figure 5.4 shows the costs of implementing protocol 2 (the sifting approach) to different depths. As shown, unlike for protocol 1, the costs of implementing protocol 2 increase substantially as greater depths are required. This is because excavating a one-foot layer of soil across the entire 7,000-acre site costs more than $250 million. Also, the multiple scans at the bottom of each excavation add to the costs.

Figure 5.4
Direct Costs of Clearing UXO According to Protocol 2, Implemented to Different Depths

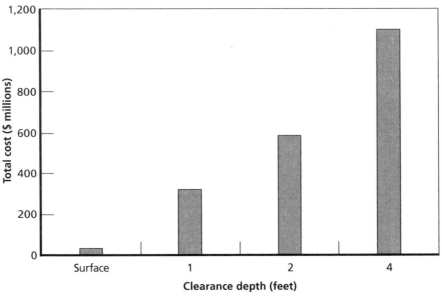

For this protocol, the costs of implementation to four feet are more than three times as high as the costs of implementation to one foot, even though 93 percent of the UXO is on the surface or in the first foot of soil. Similar results are likely at other sites because of the high costs of excavating and moving large volumes of soil.

Figure 5.5 shows the results of protocol 3 using different numbers of repeat scans. Each of our cost estimations for protocol 3 assumed that all ordnance to a depth of four feet would be cleared. As shown, increasing the number of times the site must be rescanned with metal detectors and new anomalies excavated increases the costs substantially, though the amount of increase decreases as more scans are conducted. For example, the second scan adds an additional $17 million to the total cost, the third scan adds $14 million, the fourth

Figure 5.5
Direct Costs of Protocol 3 Conducted to a Depth of Four Feet, with Different Numbers of Repeat Scans

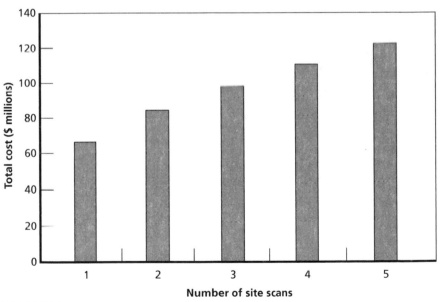

scan adds $12 million, and the fifth scan adds $10 million. Very little UXO or scrap is recovered on the last scan, but costs are incurred because of the time required to search the site. Thus the greater the number of times the site is scanned, the less will be spent on ordnance removal and destruction as compared to search time.

Figure 5.6 compares the cost differences among all three protocols, and Tables 5.5 and 5.6 summarize all the costs. As shown, the cost differences among the protocols are dramatic, especially as one increases the required depth of clearance. At the four-foot clearance level, protocol 2 (at a total cost of $1.1 billion) is 17 times as expensive as protocol 1 (which costs a total of $67 million) and 9 times as costly as the most costly version of protocol 3 (conducting five scans

Figure 5.6
Comparative Costs of the Different Clearance Protocols

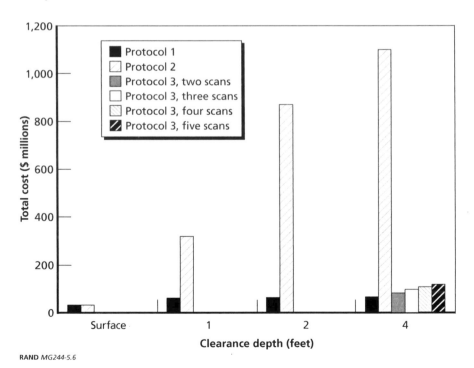

Table 5.5
Summary of Costs of Protocols 1 and 2

Depth	Protocol 1 ($ Millions)	Protocol 2 ($ Millions)
Surface	35	35
1 foot	63	320
2 feet	64	590
4 feet	67	1,100

Table 5.6
Summary of Costs of Protocol 3

Number of Full-Site Surveys with Metal Detector (Four-Foot Search Depth)	Total Cost ($ Millions)
1	67
2	84
3	98
4	110
5	120

of the entire site, which costs $120 million). Indeed, protocol 3 could yield similar results as protocol 2 in terms of public safety. If enough repeat scans are conducted, protocol 3 might ensure that all the ordnance is detected (at least within the first two feet, where 98 percent of it is located), but at far less financial cost and with far less damage to the environment. The effectiveness of repeat scans in finding UXO missed during the first scan would need to be tested, however.

Any of these protocols—even those with lower costs—will strain the historical budget for this installation. The UXO remediation budget for Site A is currently about $8 million per year. Assuming an interest rate of 5 percent, protocol 1 at a search depth of four feet would have a present-value cost of $15 million per year over 5 years or $8.6 million per year over 10 years. Costs would be essentially the same for protocol 1 implemented to a two-foot search depth ($15 million over 5 years or $8.3 million over 10 years).

Implementing protocol 2—even to two feet—is entirely infeasible given the current budget. This method would cost $140 million per year over 5 years or $80 million per year over 10 years for a two-foot UXO search and excavation. At four feet, the cost would rise to $260 million over 5 years or $150 million over 10 years. Either of these figures far exceeds the currently available budget—and indeed would consume in a single year more than the fiscal year 2004 budget of $57 million that is intended to cover all environmental cleanup costs at all Army installations across the United States closed under BRAC.

Protocol 3, while it might address the problem of remnant UXO not discovered after one scan of the site, would also exceed the current budget, though not nearly as much as protocol 2. If the site were scanned five times (an extreme proposition, but required to approach 100 percent detection of UXO), the cost per year would total $27 million for a 5-year time line or $16 million for a 10-year time line. The latter figure is double the current annual budget for UXO remediation.

Our Estimates Have Some Limitations

The results of this case study are restricted to Site A, and the estimated costs represent Site A's unique characteristics. Further, the costs represent direct costs only; actual costs would be higher due to contractor markups (which RACER can calculate). The case study is also limited by various constraints specific to RACER, some of which we could not fully address, including the following:

1. We did not address the assumption of consistent UXO remediation costs across all soil types, since RACER does not consider soil type as an input parameter in the OE Removal Action Module.

2. Likewise, while we modified RACER's assumptions about the use of backhoes by removing the backhoe rental costs for search depths of two feet or less, we were unable to account for any

changes in performance rates (such as increased manual labor time) due to the removal of this mechanical aid.

3. We were unable to fully address RACER's assumption of performance consistency across depth. That is, we could not account for cost differences associated with the need to dig deeper holes to search for deeper anomalies, although we were able to account for variations in anomaly density with depth.

Conclusion: Cleanup Protocols Are a Major Cost Driver

As is evident from the analysis in this chapter, difficult choices must be made about the tradeoff between UXO cleanup costs and the probability that UXO will remain behind after cleanup is completed. The only guaranteed way to ensure that all UXO has been removed is to excavate and sift all the soil at UXO-affected areas. At Site A, the total direct cost of this approach (without contractor markups) would exceed $1.1 billion—nearly 20 times the cost of the conventional UXO remediation approach. Even if paid in installments over a long period, this amount exceeds the entire budget allocated by Congress for cleanup of all Army BRAC installations. An alternative is to search areas of concern several times to find items left behind after the first scan (protocol 3 in our analysis). This approach could, in theory, yield probabilities of finding UXO approaching 100 percent, and even when implemented in its most stringent permutation (with five scans), it is about one-tenth as costly as sifting all the soil. However, this approach still would cost more than is currently available in the site's annual budget.

This case study illustrates that the choice of cleanup process can be perhaps the most significant cost driver of all in UXO remediation. The effects of variations in cleanup process have not been considered in previous cost estimates. In deciding how to go forward with cleanup of UXO sites, policymakers need to understand the budgetary implications of their choices.

CHAPTER SIX

Recommendations

Military base closures have focused attention on the many acres of land, once host to active training ranges, now contaminated with UXO. If they are to offer economic value, these areas must be cleaned and transferred to other federal agencies and state authorities, or sold to private interests. This process, however, has sparked many challenges—most driven by the high costs associated with remediation. At present, no widely accepted process for estimating UXO cleanup costs exists. In its absence, decisionmakers are confronted with vastly different estimates generated through divergent methods. Further, the lack of sufficient technologies for locating buried UXO has fueled a controversy over which cleanup processes are sufficient to protect the public health, while also preserving valuable environmental resources. Conflicting ideas about how UXO should be cleaned up, when combined with the paucity of necessary historical data, have made accurate cost estimation impossible. Ultimately, our analysis has demonstrated that we need better ways to estimate UXO cleanup costs—ways that are site-specific, universally used, and more accurate in modeling actual cleanup demands. The analysis has also shown that regulators' decisions—as yet uncodified—have a substantial impact on costs, as seen in the substantial cost differences resulting from different approaches to UXO clearance. At present, these decisions vary considerably and conflict with each other, further emphasizing the need for national standards that are sensitive to cost considerations as well as environmental and safety concerns.

In the absence of verified cost models and national standards for UXO remediation, costs cannot be accurately forecasted, making realistic long-term strategic planning unattainable. Such efforts are in process. For instance, DoD is developing an inventory of UXO sites with data necessary for cost estimation. But much still needs to be done in terms of cost-estimation tools and policymaking. This chapter provides brief recommendations for improving the cost-estimation and decisionmaking process, based on the analyses presented in the previous chapters.

Improve and Standardize Cost-Estimation Tools

DoD should continue its efforts to develop a uniform strategy for UXO cleanup cost estimation. In order to compare or combine cost estimates from multiple sites, the method used to obtain the cost estimate must be consistent. A feasible way to reach this goal is to modify RACER's OE Removal Action Module and establish a standardized RACER implementation method.

As noted in Chapters Four and Five, RACER 2002 has limitations. Most important, it does not

- recognize the difference in effort required for searching to different depths within specific ranges;
- consider the variable effort required for different soil types (i.e., clay, gravel, rock, sand, ferrous);
- account for the vertical distribution of UXO density across depth; and
- consider the length of time of range use, or variations in range use over time, in estimating anomaly density values.

For RACER to be used as the official standard for cost estimation, it must be modified to address these limitations and more accurately simulate the cleanup process. Critical modifications should include adding the following capabilities:

- accurate calculation of cost estimates for different search depth requirements, considering the vertical distribution of UXO and the variable effort required for excavation to different depths;
- identification of the site's soil type and the use of this information in the cost-estimation process; and
- identification of the length of time a range was used for different weapons activities and the application of this information in estimating the default anomaly density values.

Other modifications would include an option to select the method for vegetation clearance (manual, mechanical, or controlled burn) and to choose the method for ordnance excavation (backhoes or shovels). Finally, while completing the study, we noticed that the OE Removal Action Module returned to the default settings for the "Surveying" and "UXO Mapping" sections whenever a change was made to the data in the "Removal Area" section. This may confuse the user and lead to cost-estimation errors if the user does not realize that RACER has automatically reverted to the default settings.

Once initial modifications are completed, the OE Removal Action Module should be validated by checking it against actual cost data for a variety of different types of UXO sites. Then it should be modified again as necessary to correct additional limitations identified in the validation process.

Establish Baseline Standards for UXO Cleanup

Due to the multiple limitations and challenges associated with UXO remediation efforts, solving the UXO problem involves more than a simple decision to clean the land. This report has emphasized that no existing technology can guarantee that all UXO has been located. As a result, regulators and the military have had difficulty agreeing upon which UXO clearance process is sufficient to protect the public. Chapter Five illustrated the dramatic differences in cost that can result when different clearance protocols (depths, excavation amounts, number of metal detector surveys, and so on) are chosen. In the face of these high costs and given the public concern—particularly within the communities surrounding these bases—policymakers need to make resolute decisions guiding the remediation and decisionmaking process.

The federal government should designate an appropriate lead agency to establish baseline UXO remediation standards. Baseline standards are needed to end the stalemates that have arisen among regulators, community members, and the military at many installations. There are three possible ways to determine which agency should have this role:

1. The Executive Branch could propose a specific lead agency to the Congress, and Congress could then approve the choice or recommend any alternative.
2. Without involvement from Congress, the Executive Branch could designate a specific lead agency.
3. The Congress could designate a specific lead agency, without the involvement of the Executive Branch in the choice of agency but including the Executive Branch in decisions about specific policies.

Executive Branch leadership would be the fastest way to achieve the goal of designating a lead agency. However, the choice would probably be subject to legal challenges by those who disagree with the policies that the agency implements. Such challenges might prove difficult to resolve without the underpinning of laws that lay out the goals of the UXO remediation program. Comparable laws exist for other environmental contamination problems (surface water contamination is regulated under the Clean Water Act and the Safe Drinking Water Act, air pollution is regulated under the Clean Air Act, and so on). Thus, ideally, Congress would become involved. Option 1 (in which the Executive Branch proposes an agency to the Congress, and Congress then approves it or recommends an alternative) is likely to be the best because the Executive Branch can act more quickly than Congress and can help to speed congressional action.

The most likely candidates to serve as the lead agency are the Army Corps of Engineers and/or the EPA. Although the EPA generally holds regulatory authority over environmental contamination, involvement of the Army Corps of Engineers is not unprecedented. For example, the Corps and EPA have joint regulatory responsibility for safeguarding wetlands under the Clean Water Act. The Corps wrote the final regulatory definition of a wetland as well as the wetlands delineation manuals used to guide enforcement (National Research Council, 1995). The Corps has expertise in explosive ordnance detection and disposal that would be an essential asset in developing standards, whether jointly with EPA or on its own.

For most environmental contaminants, such as those in drinking water or industrial effluents, standards are based on a permissible, maximum concentration of the contaminant in the environmental medium. For example, under the Safe Drinking Water Act, the EPA has established "maximum contaminant levels" for a wide variety of chemicals found in drinking water, recognizing that achieving concentrations of zero is technically infeasible. To enforce the standards, EPA requires that water utilities periodically sample their water after it passes through the water treatment system. A similar approach to regulating UXO cleanup—that is, based on concentrations of UXO remaining after cleanup technologies have been implemented—is not possible because there is no feasible way to determine the remaining UXO concentration short of excavating the entire site and sifting it. Rather, the standards should be process oriented. They should specify the depth to which UXO should be cleared for different land uses, but should use procedural manuals to identify various options for achieving the depth requirements.

Depth and search process requirements should differ for different land uses and site conditions. For example, the policy could state that a site designated for use as a wildlife reserve that is expected to have low UXO density and a high potential for shallow, buried UXO should be cleared to one foot using one survey with a metal detector. On the other hand, the standards could require that a site with identical characteristics but with an intended use as a recreational facility be cleared to two feet, with multiple searches for UXO conducted in key areas to decrease the likelihood that ordnance is left behind. Also, the standards could specify the nature and frequency of return visits to the site to visually check for any UXO that may have migrated to the surface via frost-heave or erosion. An algorithm that considers site characteristics (UXO density, depth, and others) and future land uses could be created to guide the decisionmaking process.

The standards should provide for waivers for special situations in which the required clearance process and depth are technically or economically impractical to achieve. Environmental regulatory programs commonly include provisions for such waivers. For example, under CERCLA, waivers from usual groundwater cleanup standards are possible based on technical impracticability (National Research Council, 1994).

The standards should not specify a particular detection technology to be used. Technology is changing, and establishing technology-based standards might freeze innovation. Furthermore, the performance of detectors varies from one location to the next, so flexibility is needed in deciding which technology is best for a particular site.

Finally, the standards should specify institutional controls to be implemented after the UXO clearance process is complete. The required controls could depend on site characteristics, planned future land uses, and clearance procedure. No matter how thorough the cleanup, there will almost always remain the chance that some UXO was not detected. Standard processes are needed to convey this information to future landowners and to ensure that the information is not lost.

A significant consideration in implementing UXO remediation standards is cost. As shown in this report, UXO remediation is very expensive, and the cost varies substantially with the cleanup protocol chosen. Congress should provide appropriate direction to the designated standard-writing agency on trading off costs versus reduction in UXO risk when setting the standards. Additional studies of the cost implications of UXO response alternatives may be needed before the standards can be established.

Establish Database of UXO Incidents

The federal government should establish a publicly accessible database of UXO accidents in the United States. Ideally, the database would be maintained by the agency designated as the lead regulatory authority for UXO. As the database matures, the agency could use the information it contains to update UXO clearance standards. The database should include all domestic UXO incidents, including those that involve explosive ordnance disposal contractors and military personnel, as well as incidents involving civilians. It should also include incidents that occur off of military property; we were told that UXO incidents often occur off-site, after an unauthorized individual finds a UXO item and brings it home as a curiosity. Such a database would provide valuable new information to support future estimates of the risks of domestic UXO. In turn, improved risk estimation would improve estimates of how the risk-reduction benefits of UXO remediation compare to the costs.

References

Army Environmental Center and Army Technical Center for Explosives Safety, *Study of Ammunition Dud and Low Order Detonation Rates,* SFIM-AEC-ET-CR-200049, Army Environmental Center: Aberdeen Proving Ground, Maryland, 2000.

Crull, Michelle, Linda Taylor, and John Tipton, "Estimating Ordnance Penetration into Earth," paper presented at UXO Forum '99, May 1999. Online at https://www.denix.osd.mil/denix/Public/News/OSD/UXO/Conferences/Forum99/CS_Crull.pdf.

Defense Science Board, *Report of the Defense Science Board Task Force on Unexploded Ordnance Clearance (UXO) Clearance, Active Range UXO Clearance, and Explosive Ordnance Disposal (EOD) Programs,* Office of the Under Secretary of Defense for Acquisition and Technology, U.S. Government Printing Office: Washington, D.C., 1998. Online at http://www.acq.osd.mil/dsb/uxoandeod.pdf.

Department of Defense (DoD), "Closed, Transferred, and Transferring Ranges Containing Military Munitions: Proposed Rule," *Federal Register,* Vol. 62, No. 187 (September 26, 1997), pp. 50795–50843.

———, *Unexploded Ordnance Response: Technology and Cost,* A Report to Congress, Preliminary Draft, Washington, D.C.: Department of Defense, March 2001a.

———, *Unexploded Ordnance Response: Estimated Costs and Technology Investments,* A Report to the Congressional Defense Committees, Washington, D.C.: Department of Defense, March 2001b.

———, *Defense Environmental Restoration Program Annual Report to Congress,* Washington, D.C.: Department of Defense, April 2003.

Department of Defense and Environmental Protection Agency (DoD/EPA), *DoD and EPA Management Principles for Implementing Response Actions at Closed, Transferring, and Transferred (CTT) Ranges,* Washington, D.C.: EPA, March 2000.

DoD Explosives Safety Board (DDESB), *Department of Defense Ammunition and Explosives Safety Standards*, DOD 6055.9-STD, Washington, D.C.: Department of Defense, 1999.

Earth Tech, *RACER Quick Reference Guide* and other help manuals, Englewood, CO: Earth Tech, 2002.

Environmental Protection Agency (EPA), *Draft Handbook on the Management of Ordnance and Explosives at Closed, Transferred and Transferring Ranges,* June 2001.

————, *Used or Fired Munitions and Unexploded Ordnance at Closed, Transferred, and Transferring Military Ranges: Report and Analysis of EPA Survey Results,* EPA-505-R-00-01, September 2000. Online at http://www.peer.org/EPA/EPA_Final_UXO_Report.pdf (as of May 6, 2003).

Fields, Timothy, Jr., letter to Ms. Sherri W. Goodman, Deputy Under Secretary of Defense (Environmental Security), Department of Defense, Washington, D.C., April 22, 1999.

General Accounting Office (GAO), *Environmental Liabilities: DoD Training Cleanup Cost Estimates Are Likely Understated,* GAO-01-479, Washington, D.C.: GAO, April 2001.

————, *Military Base Closures: Progress in Completing Actions from Prior Realignments and Closures,* GAO-02-433, Washington, D.C.: GAO, April 2002a.

————, *Environmental Contamination, Corps Needs to Reassess Its Determinations That Many Former Defense Sites Do Not Need Cleanup,* Report to Congressional Requesters, GAO-02-658, Washington, D.C.: GAO, August 2002b.

Jaffe, Harry, "Spring Valley as Ground Zero," *Washingtonian,* Vol. 33, No. 3 (December 2000), pp. 121–129.

Jenkins, Tom F., A. D. Hewitt, M. E. Walsh, T. A. Ranney, J. C. Pennington, S. Thiboutot, G. Ampleman, and M. H. Stutz, "Explosives Contamination at DoD Firing Ranges," paper presented at UXO/Countermine Forum, Orlando, FL, September 3–6, 2002.

Lauritzen, Erik, "The Challenge of Demilitarisation and Disposal of Ammunition," *Military Technology*, Vol. 25, No. 7 (2001), pp. 34–39.

MacDonald, Jacqueline, J. R. Lockwood, John McFee, Thomas Altshuler, Thomas Broach, Lawrence Carin, Russell Harmon, Carey Rappaport, Waymond Scott, and Richard Weaver, *Alternatives for Landmine Detection*, Santa Monica, CA: RAND Corporation, MR-1608-OSTP, 2003.

MacDonald, Jacqueline, Debra Knopman, J. R. Lockwood, Gary Cecchine, and Henry Willis, *Risks of Unexploded Ordnance: Critical Review of Assessment Methods*, Santa Monica, CA: RAND Corporation, MR-1674-A, 2004.

MacDonald, Jacqueline, Debra Knopman, Noreen Clancy, Jimmie McEver, and Henry Willis, *Transferring Army BRAC Lands Containing Unexploded Ordnance: Lessons Learned and Future Options*, Santa Monica, CA: RAND Corporation, MG-199-A, 2005.

National Research Council, *Alternatives for Ground Water Cleanup*, Washington, D.C.: National Academy Press, 1994.

———, *Wetlands: Characteristics and Boundaries*, Washington, D.C.: National Academy Press, 1995.

Nielson, Greg, "Spring Valley, Washington, DC: Formerly Used Defense Site," paper delivered at the UXO Forum 2002, Orlando, FL, September 3–6, 2002.

Occupational Safety and Health Administration, U.S. Department of Labor, Regulations (Standards-29 CFR), Specific Excavation Requirements (1926.651[j]), October 31, 1989, as amended August 9, 1994.

"Old Firing Range Swept for Shells After Two Die," *New York Times*, January 20, 1984, p. A13.

Parsons Engineering Science, Inc., *Ordnance Detection and Discrimination Study* (ODDS), Final Report, prepared for the U.S. Army Corps of Engineers, January 2002.

Peterson, Jim, and Kate Peterson, "Estimating Budget Costs for Ordnance and Explosive Projects Using RACER," briefing presented at RACER training session, Earth Tech, Englewood, CO, April 2001.

PricewaterhouseCoopers, *RACER Accreditation Recommendation*, Greely, CO: PricewaterhouseCoopers, LLC, July 2001. Online at http://www.afcesa.af.mil/ces/cesc/cost_engr/documents/vvafinal.pdf.

U.S. Army Corps of Engineers (USACE), "Ordnance and Explosives Response," EP110-1-18, April 2000.

———, "Basic Safety Concepts and Considerations for OE Operations," Engineering Pamphlet 385-1-95a, June 29, 2001.

———, *Development of a Database for Ordnance Related Civilian Accidents: Final Report,* DACA87-00-0-0048 D.O. #0002, Huntsville, AL: Army Corps of Engineers, 2003a.

———, "Formerly Utilized Defense Sites," September 30, 2003b. Online at www.hq.environmental.usace.army.mil.

U.S. Department of Defense—see Department of Defense.

U.S. Environmental Protection Agency—see Environmental Protection Agency.

U.S. General Accounting Office—see General Accounting Office.

Woolford, James, EPA Federal Facilities Restoration and Reuse Office, letter to Mr. Art Fraas, Office of Management and Budget, March 22, 2000.